How to Choose Your Major

How to Choose Your Major

Mary E. Ghilani

GREENWOOD™

An Imprint of ABC-CLIO, LLC

Santa Barbara, California • Denver, Colorado

Library of Congress Cataloging-in-Publication Data

Names: Ghilani, Mary E., 1958– author.
Title: How to choose your major / Mary E. Ghilani.
Description: Santa Barbara, California : Greenwood, [2017] | Includes
    bibliographical references and index.
Identifiers: LCCN 2017010832 (print) | LCCN 2017026997 (ebook) |
    ISBN 9781440856631 (ebook) | ISBN 9781440856624 (alk. paper)
Subjects: LCSH: College majors—United States. | College students—
    Vocational guidance—United States.
Classification: LCC LB2361.5 (ebook) | LCC LB2361.5 .G55 2017 (print) |
    DDC 378.2/41—dc23
LC record available at https://lccn.loc.gov/2017010832

ISBN: 978-1-4408-5662-4
EISBN: 978-1-4408-5663-1

21 20 19 18 17   1 2 3 4 5

This book is also available as an eBook.

Greenwood
An Imprint of ABC-CLIO, LLC

ABC-CLIO, LLC
130 Cremona Drive, P.O. Box 1911
Santa Barbara, California 93116–1911
www.abc-clio.com

This book is printed on acid-free paper ∞

Manufactured in the United States of America

Contents

Acknowledgments

Although writing is often considered a solitary activity, no book is written in isolation. Having said that, I'd like to acknowledge the assistance of the following people:

Thanks to Dr. Janet E. Wall, CEUOnestop.com, for her helpful suggestions to improve the book.

Dr. Spencer Niles, dean and professor, School of Education, The College of William & Mary, for editing the "Hope-Centered Model of Career Development" section.

Shirley Yanovich, chair of the CIS program at Luzerne County Community College, for editing the "Career Opportunities in the Computer Industry" chart.

Dr. Frank Derby, chair of Surveying Engineering Program at Penn State University, and Dr. Charles Ghilani, Professor Emeritus, Surveying Engineering at Penn State, for providing an excellent definition of Surveying Engineering.

Mia Bassham, director of the Library at Luzerne County Community College and Kate Cummings, Electronic Resource Librarian at Luzerne County Community College, for reviewing the section on Library Science for accuracy.

Lori Major, CPA, professor at Luzerne County Community College, for reviewing the section on accounting for accuracy.

Barbara Bissonnette, principal of Forward Motion Coaching, for providing some useful tips to help Asperger's students choose a major.

Margaret Krantz, director of Hanover College Career Center, for granting permission to reprint the *Liberal Arts Skills at Work* skills charts.

Thanks to the student, whose name I unfortunately can't recall, who first asked me about "careers for compassionate people," which I later used as the title for Chapter 5.

And finally, heartfelt thanks, always, to my husband, Chuck, who supported me in whatever endeavor I wanted to pursue.

Introduction

When I was in the seventh grade, I knew that I wanted to become a veterinarian. Two semesters into college, my grade-point average made it painfully clear that I would have to give up my dream of becoming a vet. So I switched majors and switched majors again until I eventually ended up with a master's degree in speech pathology. To make a long story short, I was unhappy with my career choice and spent the next several years bumping along in a variety of different jobs. After years of soul-searching, I decided to complete a master's degree in counseling and eventually landed my current job as director of career services at our local community college. I remember making the very conscious choice, at 46 years old, to pursue what I knew best—career counseling. My husband tells people that I became a career counselor because I changed my major so many times.

Everyone has stories like mine—of going to college for one thing and ending up being something else. Very few people in this world wake up one morning with the idea to become a surgeon and actually end up being a surgeon until they retire. Recent economic events have made staying in one job or career throughout one's life almost impossible because of technology changes, layoffs, and other unforeseen factors in one's life.

There are even some examples of famous people who changed their careers and, I might add, ended up having very successful lives:

Andrea Bocelli was a lawyer. After graduating with a law degree from the University of Pisa, Andrea Bocelli worked as a defense attorney until the age of 34, when he left his job to sing full time.[1]

Joy Behar was a high school English teacher. The host of *The View* and *The Joy Behar Show* wasn't always the comedian we all love. In fact, Behar was a high school English teacher until the age of 40.[2]

Julia Child wasn't cooking during World War II—she was working for the OSS (the predecessor of today's CIA) as a spy. She went on clandestine missions to China and Sri Lanka (known as Ceylon) to give intelligence documents to agents in the field. She didn't enter cooking school until age 36.[3]

Sheryl Crow majored in music education and taught elementary school in St. Louis after she graduated from college. She sang in bands on the weekends and later moved to Los Angeles to join the music industry.[4]

Given the circuitous nature of careers, I am amazed at how early in a person's life we're asked to make such an important decision—what we want to be when we grow up.

College students used to feel less anxiety about choosing and declaring a major at the end of their sophomore year of college. Students today start to feel the pressure of choosing a major much earlier on in their academic careers. High school students agonize over their potential college majors, often as a result of good-intentioned parents or advisors attempting to shepherd young people toward a course of study that will lead to a vocation and employment after graduation. College is increasingly seen as a place to professionalize, leaving students to feel as though they must pick a major without delay.

Most high school students are not ready to make decisions about a career and a major because they have been exposed only to a limited number of occupations. They know about the field of education from their teachers, and a little bit about their parent's occupations. With colleges offering hundreds of majors to choose from, high school and college students often find the process of "deciding what they should do for the rest of their life," an overwhelming task. They often start out with one idea, dump that, adopt another idea, and dump that, all to the frustration of their parents, friends, and relatives.

If you are in high school, you probably have not accumulated enough work experience to be able to identify what your work values and attitudes are. You may not even realize the full extent of your abilities yet. Some people have talents that, for one reason or other, surface only later in life. Even many college students aren't ready to declare a major simply because they do not have enough information to make a realistic career decision.

Over the past 20 plus years, I've been a college academic advisor, a career counselor for a grant program that connected technical careers in high school to college, and the director of career services at a community college. About half of the students I see in the career center need some kind of help deciding on their major. Some students are totally clueless about what they want to do, while others have it narrowed down to one or two occupations and just need more factual information about duties, salary, and employment prospects before being able to make a decision. I see traditional-aged students just out of high school; single parents trying to improve their lives; and older adults who have decided to come back to school because of unemployment, divorce, or the desire for a career change. All of them want to know "what can I do with a major in . . ." and more importantly, "Can I get a job with that major?"

How to Choose Your Major is written for anyone who hasn't figured out what to major in . . . yet.

CHAPTER ONE

College Is a Major Deal

The best way to predict the future is to plan it.

—Peter Drucker

Each fall, about 2.1 million (69.2%) high school students enroll in college—an enrollment rate that has been steady for the past couple of years. More women (72.6%) than men (65.8%) are enrolled in college, and about two in three of those high school graduates who enroll in college attend four-year colleges.[1]

Despite the conversations in the media about the value of a college education, the data is clear that education is becoming a necessity. According to the Bureau of Labor Statistics (BLS), "The unemployment rate for recent high school graduates not enrolled in college was 20.7 percent, higher than the rate of 12.6 percent for recent graduates enrolled in college."[2]

While it's true that jobs are back after our recent recession, Anthony Carnevale, Tamara Jayasundera, and Artem Gulish write in *America's Divided Recovery: College Haves and Have-Nots*, "They are not the same jobs that were lost during the recession. The great Recession decimated low-skill blue-collar and clerical jobs, whereas the recovery added primarily high-skill managerial and professional jobs."[3] They state that workers with a bachelor's degree or higher now make up a larger share of the workforce (36%) than workers with a high school diploma or less (34%).[4] Georgetown University's Center on Education and the Workforce statistics show that by 2020, 65 percent of all jobs in the United States will require education beyond a high school diploma.[5]

The Value of Earning Your Degree

Many people are reconsidering the merits of a college degree. They are wondering if the expensive tuition and amount of student loan debt is worth it in the future. Here are some reasons why earning your degree is *still* worthwhile:

1. **College graduates usually earn more money** during their working lives than people with only high school diplomas. A 2014 Pew research study revealed that "millennial college graduates ages 25 to 32 who are working full time earn more annually—about $17,500 more than employed young adults holding only a high school diploma."[6] Furthermore, "the U.S. Census Bureau has reported that those with bachelor's degrees earn nearly 2 million dollars, associate's degrees nearly 1.5 million dollars, and high school diplomas nearly 1.2 million dollars during their careers."[7]

2. **A college degree will make you more marketable.** Employers like to hire college graduates because college graduates can think and learn. Graduates with two- or four-year degrees qualify for a greater range of higher-paying entry- and upper-level career positions than those with only a high school degree. Earning a college degree can open doors that would otherwise remain closed.

3. **Are you really that much smarter if you earn a college degree?** In general, the answer is "yes." Most college graduates come away with a greater knowledge base and an ability to problem-solve and think analytically, which are all very attractive qualities to a potential employer.

4. **Attending college provides professional networking opportunities** that are not available to those who don't go to college. Many professional organizations have student chapters on college that provide valuable networking opportunities with professionals in a student's chosen field.

5. **Graduates reap other benefits from going to college**. Some of the greatest benefits of a college education are the experiences that you gain while attending school. For example, you have the opportunity to meet new people from all over the world and to expand your knowledge base by being introduced to theories and concepts you might not have learned about anywhere else.[8]

All of us have heard those alarming stories about college students who cannot find a job and have mountains of debt loan. Some of these instances may be real, but the media tend to exaggerate the problem. According to the College Board, about 60 percent of students who earned bachelor's degrees in 2012–2013 from the public and private nonprofit institutions borrowed an average of $27,300,[9] which is a tiny fraction of the long-term economic benefits of college. According to the College Board, "In 2014–15, full-time students receive an average of about $6,110 in grant aid and education tax benefits at public four-year institutions, $5,090 at public two-year colleges, and $18,870 at private nonprofit four-year institutions to help them pay the published prices."[10] The unemployment rate in April 2015 for people between 25 and 34 years old with a bachelor's degree was a mere 3 percent. Community college students do not graduate with huge amounts of debt because tuition costs are low. Many *can* find a job after graduation or choose to continue their studies at a four-year school because their credits are transferrable. Comparing the cost of going to college with the cost of not having any education, college will always be a better deal and, in most situations, will help you be more successful in life. The bottom line is that a college degree is a good investment in your future.

Future Employability

In the old model of work (which wasn't that long ago), the employer provided job security through lifelong employment. Today, long-term job security has been replaced with the concept of "employability." Career development and advancement used to be guaranteed, but now each employee is responsible for his or her career growth and advancement.

Likewise, the modern career development path is now defined as multidirectional rather than linear. Today, career development is characterized by starts and stops, detours, and job mobility across multiple employers. According to the Bureau of Labor Statistics, "The average worker currently holds ten different jobs before age forty, and this number is projected to grow."[11] In addition, "Forrester Research predicts that today's youngest workers (that's you) will hold twelve to fifteen jobs in their lifetime."[12]

As a college career counselor, I've observed a definite shift in student attitude regarding the choice of major. When I was in high school, the mantra was, "Go to college and life will be good." And this is still pretty good advice today. We know that college graduates certainly do better over their lifetime than those with only a high school diploma. But in today's world, a four-year degree is no longer a guaranteed ticket to a well-paying job or economic security. During our recent recession, students saw their parents and family members suddenly lose their jobs after being with a company for 25 years or more. The students whom I now see, those who have experienced our latest recession, talk less about finding their "passion" and more about finding a "good" or "stable" job that will support themselves and a family.

Many career development professionals believe that we should be focused on preparing for a "career," not just a "job." In this model, work is a lifelong journey that evolves as we personally and professionally grow and experience new things. If you view your job as just a "job," then your opportunities are restricted by the confines of whatever organization employs you. Viewing a job as a stepping stone on a lifelong career journey will encourage you to advance and accumulate new skills—all of the things that employers desire in an employee. You will no longer be limited by your current job—your career journey will involve moving on to another company that offers a better environment, a higher salary, or a chance for promotion, or it may involve going back to school, picking up a new certification, or changing careers altogether. This lifelong approach will not only help you become a valuable asset for an employer but will also better prepare you for a work environment in which career upheavals occur without warning.

What's Your Major?

How do most college students choose a major? In 2013 the National Association of Colleges and Employers (NACE) surveyed students about what motivated them to choose their major. Forty-five percent of those surveyed believed that their major led to a career, and 35.6 percent chose their major because of the appeal of the subject matter. Surprisingly, "getting a job immediately after graduation was *not* a top reason. However the chance for income and the chance for employment were the reasons 16 percent of the respondents gave for selecting a major."[13] Another study by Christopher G. Takacs, a graduate student in sociology at the University of Chicago, and Daniel F. Chambliss, a professor of sociology at Hamilton College, found that students were more likely to major in a field if they had an inspiring and caring faculty member in the first class in their field.[14] Students were just as likely to write off a field just based on a single negative experience with a professor. Takacs and Chambliss call this phenomenon "majoring in a professor."[15]

If you don't have a major yet, you might not know how to respond to the most commonly asked question of all college students, "What's your major?" There are many reasons for career indecision—maybe you haven't had a chance to explore all of the hundreds of opportunities available. Or maybe you're someone who has such broad or varied interests that you don't want to limit yourself to just one area. If you are undecided about your future career plans, you may think you're the only one in your class who hasn't selected a major. According to David K. Moldoff, founder of AcademyOne, "Twenty percent of college freshmen enroll as 'undecided', making it one of the most popular majors. In addition, many transfer students change their fields of study two, three, or even four times during their college career."[16]

The good news is that college is the perfect opportunity to explore majors and careers. Your core classes will give you an opportunity to sample fields of study from art to philosophy. That's why they're required. In addition, you will have access to professors who are experts in their professional fields; exposure to jobs through internships and service-learning activities; access to employer presentations, job fairs, and other services provided by your career services office.

"Exploratory" Is the New Undeclared

When I worked for a large, four-year public university, the "undecided" major was the largest major on campus. To quell the anxiety students (and their parents) had about "having to choose a major," we stressed that it was "okay" to be "undecided"—that your freshman and sophomore years were the appropriate time to explore courses and interests.

Back in 2009, John Krumboltz, a noted career theorist, wrote, "The adjective *undecided* seems to have a negative connotation in our society. Politicians who change their mind on an issue are labeled *wishy-washy* or a *flip-flopper.* So if you are undecided about your future (as indeed every sensible person should be), don't call yourself undecided, call yourself openminded. You'll get more respect even though the two terms mean the same thing."[17]

Today, many colleges are moving away from the negative-sounding "undecided" label to encourage students to explore courses and learn about new disciplines. Exploration is encouraged and normalized, instead of referring to indecision as aimless drifting. College students are encouraged to regard uncertainty about their college major as a normal process. Some experts believe that allowing students to take their time in exploring majors may actually help them make better career choices.

When to Choose a Major

When is the best time to choose a major? Do you have to know before you begin college, or is it better to wait until your junior year to choose a major? Colleges and universities would like to see students declare a major early because retention rates are better and students are more likely to graduate in four years. On the other hand, college administrators also recognize that deciding on a major can be overwhelming, especially when coupled with the fear that a wrong choice will result in added semesters and increased college debt.

Professionals in academia debate about this issue. The trouble with most traditional baccalaureate curriculums is that you don't get a real taste of your major until your junior year. By then, you've already invested two years of coursework that may not be relevant if you decide to switch to an unrelated major. To combat this issue, many schools have instituted a required freshman orientation course in their major to help students determine if they are in the right major. Associate degrees, on the other hand, have the advantage of having major courses in the first or second semester of their curriculum. Students know almost immediately if they're going to like or not like their major.

To answer the question of when to choose a major, ideally it's better to choose a major earlier rather than later, but (and here's the caveat) it really depends on the requirements of the major that you choose. Some majors are more lenient than others in accepting students into their programs at any level of education. Others are not. For example, one of the colleges in my area admits only first-time freshman into their physical therapy program. So if you're a student in your sophomore or junior who decides that you want to become a physical therapist, you'll have to go elsewhere to find another college that will admit you into its undergraduate or graduate physical therapy program.

Choosing a Science versus a Nonscience Track

If you simply cannot decide on a major, my advice is to try to choose between a science-oriented major and a nonscience one. The reason for this is that it's easier to switch from a science-based major (math, engineering, science, business, and agriculture) to a nonscience major (arts, communications, education—except math or science education and liberal arts) than it is the other way around. Science-based majors require a completely different sequence of courses (i.e., more math and science courses) than nonscience-based majors, which usually require more liberal arts and language courses.

To make matters even more complicated, some colleges have "entrance-to-major" requirements for highly competitive majors. In a previous position I was an academic advisor at a public, four-year college. To qualify for entrance into engineering, students were required to complete chemistry, calculus, and physics with a grade of "C" or better before the end of their fourth semester. In addition, each engineering major required a minimum grade-point average that changed each year depending on the size of the applicant pool.

If you start with a more academically rigorous track and then choose a major like chemistry or physics in your junior or senior year, you may only be looking at one or two additional semesters to complete your degree. If you began in a liberal arts sequence and *then* decided to switch to chemistry, you may be looking at two to three additional years to complete your degree because of the science and math prerequisites that you missed in your freshman and sophomore years.

Competitive majors (e.g., nursing, music, engineering, business) usually have a curriculum that follows a tight sequence of courses. Being admitted into a competitive major in your junior or senior years may not be possible because of missed entrance to major requirements. In the worst-case scenario, you may have to transfer to another school or find another major. It's always easier to switch *out* of engineering, for example, than it is to enter engineering (if that's even possible) later in your college career. That's why making this very basic career decision (a science-based versus a nonmath-based major) can save you time, money, and aggravation in the long run.

Courses to Take If You're Undecided

Although I stated earlier that it was better to decide on a major earlier, rather than later, the problem is that the career decision-making process is developmental in nature. That means that it takes time and every student matures at a different rate. That's why some students enter college knowing exactly what they want to major in, and others are unsure or aren't ready to make a decision.

So what should you do if you haven't decided on a major? Here are some suggestions:

1. Begin by taking the basic "core" courses—English, history, psychology, philosophy, sociology, and physical education. If you are placed in developmental math or English, begin taking that course.

2. Take courses that are common to both (or more) of the majors that you're considering. Work closely with your academic advisor each time you register for classes.

3. "Test" a possible major by taking an introductory course in whatever major interests you. Sometimes the only way to find out if you are going to enjoy accounting or graphic design is to take the course.

4. Determining which math and science courses to select will depend on what major you are interested in pursuing. If you can't decide between two majors, follow the curriculum with the most rigorous sequence of courses. For example, if major A requires biology and chemistry and major B only requires biology, then take biology *and* chemistry so you can keep both options open until you're ready to make a decision. Even though you may end up taking some extra courses that you may not need, the safest way to keep all of your options open is to prepare yourself for both (or more) majors. If you choose your courses wisely, you can always use those extra courses to fulfill the requirements for a minor or even a double major.

5. Go to your college career center and make an appointment to take an interest inventory. Continue to research career options and explore classes in majors that you think you might enjoy.

Corey

Corey was a first-semester freshman who was taking general (core) courses. Although he was undecided regarding his major, he had a couple of ideas: criminal justice, accounting, and dentistry. When it came time to preregister for courses for the upcoming spring semester, Corey didn't know what to do. In a panic, he stopped into the career center on campus. After researching some possible majors of interest, he was able to narrow his choices down to criminal justice and dentistry. For the spring semester he planned to take an introductory criminal justice course to see if he liked it. The rest of his courses were centered on common requirements for both majors. Because the science and math requirements for dentistry (essentially a premed program) were more rigorous than what were required for criminal justice, he decided to also take biology and precalculus, which resulted in a spring schedule of intro to criminal justice, precalculus, introductory biology with a lab, history II, and intro to sociology.

You Can Always Change Your Major

Switching your major in college is so common that it's almost expected. According to Virginia Gordon in her book, *The Undecided College Student: An Academic and Career Advising Challenge*, an estimated 20 to 50 percent of students enter college as "undecided" and 75 percent change their major before graduating.[18] Those statistics haven't really changed today. In "College Students Tend to Change Majors When They Find the One They Really Love," Yuritzy Ramos writes, "According to the National Center for Education Statistics, about 80 percent of students in the United States end up changing their major at least once, on average, and college students change their major at least three times over the course of their college career."[19]

Changing majors is one of the more common reasons that students take longer to finish college. A report from Complete College America, a nonprofit group based in Indianapolis, found that only 5 percent of community college students graduate with two-year degrees in two years and about 36 percent of four-year flagship public university students graduate in four years.[20] At nonflagship four-year public universities, the on-time graduation rate is 19 percent.[21]

If you are undecided, decide to switch majors, or even elect to double major, you may need to make up missed undergraduate courses plus complete the required upper-level courses for your new major. Either way, the result is that you'll be going to school longer than you planned. If you are undecided about your major, work with your advisor or see a career counselor in your college career center. If you decide to change your major even after you have already declared one, work closely with your academic advisor—they know the inside nuances about which courses are offered in what semester and how to best catch up.

Many people get upset about having to go to school for more than four years, but again, it's far better to change your mind, extend your college career, and graduate in something you like, rather than graduate in four years in a major that you do not enjoy or will never use.

What Classes Do I Take in High School?

Rule of thumb: If you are planning to go to college, take as many English, math, and science courses in high school as you can. *More is better.* If you are thinking about a science or engineering field, also take calculus and physics.

In general, students are best prepared to meet entrance requirements into a four-year college if they take the following:

- Four years of English including one unit each in composition and literature
- Three years of science (choose from biology, chemistry, and physics)
- Three years of math (algebra I, algebra II, and geometry). Some programs require trig and calculus

- Three years in any combination of arts (art, music, theater), humanities, or social studies (history, government, economics, geography, and psychology)
- Two years of world language, other than English

Recommended High School Classes for Specific College Majors

Agricultural Sciences, Horticulture, Wildlife, and Fisheries

- Science (biology I, biology II, chemistry)
- Math (algebra I, algebra II, and geometry)

Art, Architecture

- Science (choose any three from biology, ecology, environmental science, etc.)
- Math (algebra I, algebra II, and geometry)
- Art (drawing or painting classes)

(*Note*: Drafting is more relevant to architectural engineering.)

Biology, Genetics, Environmental Science, Meteorology

- Science (biology I, biology II, chemistry I, and physics)
- Math (algebra I, algebra II, geometry, and trig)

(Take as much math as possible including calculus.)

Business, Information Science

- Science (choose any three from biology, ecology, environmental science, etc.)
- Math (algebra I, algebra II, geometry, and trig)
- Electives such as accounting, into to computers, or computer applications, if possible

(If you're interested in computer science, see later.)

Chemistry, Chemical Engineering, Pharmacy

- Science (biology I, chemistry I, chemistry II, and physics)
- Math (algebra I, algebra II, geometry, and trig)

(Take as much math as possible including Calculus.)

Communications, Journalism

- Science (choose any three from biology, ecology, environmental science, etc.)
- Math (algebra I, algebra II, and geometry)
- English (creative writing, speech, and journalism)

(Take photography if interested in photojournalism; join the debate club if interested in public relations or speech communication.)

Computer Science

- Science (choose any three from biology, ecology, environmental science, etc.)
- Math (algebra I, algebra II, geometry, and trig)

(Take as much math as possible including calculus. Take electives such as computer programming courses, if offered at your high school.)

Education

- Science (choose any three from biology, ecology, environmental science, etc.)
- Math (algebra I, algebra II, and geometry)
- Social science (history, government, sociology, psychology, economics)

(Take art or music classes if you plan to be an art or music teacher. Take child care and development classes if you're interested in early childhood education. If you are interested in being a high school science or math teacher, take as many science and math classes as possible.)

Engineering

- Science (biology, chemistry, physics—take as much chemistry and physics as possible)

(If you are interested in bioengineering, take biology II also.)

- Math (algebra I, algebra II, geometry, trig)

(Take as much math as possible including calculus. Take electives in drafting, AutoCAD, computer programming or applications, if possible.)

Health Care (Physical Therapy, Nursing, Speech Pathology, etc.)

- Science (biology I, biology II, chemistry)
- Math (algebra I, algebra II, geometry)

Liberal Arts (Psychology, Sociology, History, Prelaw)

- Science (choose any three from biology, ecology, environmental science, etc.)
- Math (algebra I, algebra II, and geometry)
- Social science, arts, humanities (choose as many as possible from history, government, sociology, psychology, economics, art, music, and theater)
- Foreign language (at least two years)

(Take as many English courses as possible [literature, writing, speech]. If you're interested in law, join the debate club.)

Science, Premed, Prevet

- Science (biology I, biology II, chemistry I, physics)
- Math (algebra I, algebra II, geometry, trig, calculus)

(Take as many math and science courses as possible.)

CHAPTER TWO

How to Choose a Career

Choose a job you love and you will never have to work a day in your life.

—Confucius

Career Development Is a Process

Career development is a very personal, individualized process that often continues throughout a person's life. The career development process begins in grade school. It starts with exploring your interests and learning about careers and work opportunities. When you enter college, you test out majors through classes, internships, and summer jobs. After college, you begin your first professional job and then advance in your career, get another job, or change gears and go in another career direction. Every experience you have throughout your life—through school, hobbies, work, and the people you meet—helps define where you want to go next. The nature of career development is a dynamic and evolving process. Very few people come into this world knowing exactly what they want to do, get there, and then happily remain in their chosen profession until they retire. Many people have the unfortunate experience of discovering that what they *thought* a career was going to be and what it actually *is* are two entirely different things. Most people have to search, make mistakes, and go through several bad job experiences before finding the one that is right.

One of the hardest things to understand is that career development is a *process*, and processes take time to develop. Because career development occurs at different rates of speed, not everyone is ready to make a career choice when he or she enters college. That's why some students enter college seemingly knowing exactly what they want to major in, and others don't have a clue.

Career exploration and decision-making is the process of discovering who you are; identifying and exploring career options; and selecting an appropriate major or career based on your interests, abilities, values, and personality type. There are basically four sequential steps in the career development process:

1) **Self-assessment** (*Who am I?*)
2) **Career exploration** (*Where am I going?*)
3) **Action plan** (*How do I get there?*)
4) **Career management** (*How do I maintain my career?*)

It is important to understand that the process is *not* linear, and you may find yourself going back and forth and recycling through these stages as you make adjustments to your career plans in college and throughout your life.

Where are you in the career development process? Select the stage from the following list that best describes where you are in the career decision-making process:

Stage 1. Not a clue—no idea of what I want to do.

Stage 2. I have some idea of what I want to do but need more information about careers in general.

Stage 3. I know what I like but don't know what I can do with it (don't know what kind of job I can get).

Stage 4. I have it narrowed down to two or three majors but haven't made a decision yet (or can't decide between two majors).

Stage 5. I know what I want to major in but need more information about what I can do with it (what kind of job I can get) after I graduate.

Stage 6. I have decided on a major and know what kind of job/career it will lead to.

Everyone wants the career decision-making process to happen *yesterday*. Students want to know what to major in now because they have to register for classes for the next semester or because they feel the pressure from parents. But most of the urgency to pick a major is because they feel like something's wrong with them because, as one student recently told me, "all of my friends know what they want to major in." Well, maybe they do, and maybe they don't. Students come into my office wanting me to give them the answer, but I can't tell them what to do with the rest of their lives—as much as I'd like to help them out. It just doesn't work that way. Choosing a career involves figuring out where you fit in the world of work. And that process requires self-reflection and insight. Take the time to invest in yourself and make your own decision. It's your future, not anyone one else's. In the long run, you'll feel more certain about a well thought-out decision rather than one made under pressure.

As was alluded to earlier, career planning doesn't end when you graduate from college—it continues throughout your work life. You will graduate, get a job, and then begin the process of moving from one job to another until you retire (or die). As you grow and develop as a person, you may find yourself going through the career exploring and planning steps several times as your interests, skills, and values change. The changing job market will also have a positive or negative affect on your career plans. Career development, like life, involves growing and developing and adapting the best we can to the events that occur in our lives.

Perhaps the only truism about career development is that you *will* change your mind at some point in your career. This is normal. Some research statistics claim that people will change jobs five to seven times, and occupations three to four times, during a work life that may last forty years or more. That is not necessarily due to lack of direction but in response to changing times or personal situations. People are complex and dynamic beings. Most of us start out with one idea of what we want to do and then change and refine that idea over the course of our lives. That's why career development is a *process*—not an absolute.

Career Development Theories

You may be wondering how people go about choosing a major. In the world of career development, just as in the field of psychology, there are a variety of theories. Some of the most popular theories will be described in this section. Read them and see which ones best apply to you and your career development experiences.

John Holland's Theory of Vocational Personalities and Work Environments

John Holland, PhD, a psychologist who devoted his professional life to researching issues related to career choice and satisfaction, developed a widely used theory that basically says that people are happier and more successful in jobs that match their interest, values, and skills. According to the theory, there are six basic personality types in the workplace and six corresponding work environments.[1] For example, an individual with a social personality type will be happier and more successful if he or she chooses a job or occupation that involves interacting with people on a daily basis. In contrast, a realistic personality type will be happier in occupations that involve *doing things* (working with their hands, athletics, training animals) rather than working directly with people. The six personality types are commonly displayed as a hexagram. The types closest to each other on the hexagon have the most in common; those across from each other have the least in common. Many standardized career interest inventories (aka career assessments) are based on John Holland's theory of vocational personalities and work environments.

The following are descriptions of John Holland's six personality types. As you read through each type, ask yourself which type best describes you and your interests. You might see yourself in more than one type. Most people are a combination of more than one type, just as most occupations are made up of a combination of more than one type. Try to identify your primary and secondary types as you read through each of the descriptions.

(Descriptions are based on Holland's Occupational Themes from the Staff Development and Professional Services Web site from the University of California, Davis.[2])

Realistic—The "Doers"

Realistic individuals enjoy hands-on activities such as repairing, building, mechanics, operating machinery, and athletics. They often prefer to work with things rather than ideas and people. They enjoy engaging in physical activity and like being outdoors and working with plants and animals. People who fall into this theme generally prefer to "learn by doing" in a practical, task-oriented setting, as opposed to spending extended periods of time in a classroom. Typical realistic careers include those in the trades, athletics, military and protective services, working with animals and plants, and working outdoors.

Investigative—The "Thinkers"

Investigative individuals are often analytical, intellectual, and enjoy research, mathematical, or scientific activities. They are drawn to abstract challenges. People who fall into this theme enjoy using logic and solving highly complex problems. Typical investigative careers include biologist, chemist, physicist, medical technologist, computer systems analyst, mathematician, engineer, and other medical or research related professions.

Artistic—The "Creators"

Artistic individuals are often original, intuitive, imaginative, and enjoy creative activities such as composing or playing music, writing, drawing or painting, and acting in or directing stage productions. They enjoy self-expression through artistic creation. People who fall into this category do not like convention and conformity, but prefer flexibility. They value aesthetics, view themselves as creative and non-conforming, and appreciate or possess musical, dramatic, artistic, or writing abilities. Typical artistic careers include musician, composer, writer, artist, interior decorator, and actor.

Social—The "Helpers"

Social individuals are concerned with the welfare of others and enjoy helping, training, counseling, or developing others. Social types value relationships with others and enjoy working as part of a team. Because they genuinely enjoy working with people, they are empathetic and communicate in a warm and tactful manner. They view themselves as understanding, helpful, and skilled in teaching. Typical social careers include teacher, counselor, social worker, minister, and human resources professional.

Enterprising—The "Persuaders"

Enterprising individuals are often energetic, ambitious, adventurous, and self-confident. They enjoy activities that involve persuading others and often seek out leadership roles. They are effective public speakers and are generally sociable. They view themselves as assertive, self-confident, and skilled in leadership and public speaking. Typical enterprising careers include sales, marketing, politics, and business.

Conventional—The "Organizers"

Conventional individuals are efficient, exact, organized, and conscientious. They are comfortable working within an established chain of command. They prefer organized, systematic activities and do not like ambiguity. They are thorough, persistent, and reliable. Conventional types view themselves as responsible, orderly, efficient and possessing administrative, organizational, and numerical abilities. Typical conventional careers include administrative assistant, accountant, bookkeeper, copyeditor, health information specialist, and office manager.

Which type best describes you? Are you a doer, thinker, creator, helper, persuader, or organizer?

Happenstance Theory

Many professionals, if you were to talk to them about their career path, will say they "stumbled" into their major during college or later in life. This phenomenon has been called the "accident theory" by Bandura in 1982 and later evolved into the *happenstance theory of learning* developed by John D. Krumboltz at Stanford University.[3] In this theory, individuals "accidently" find out about a major they previously never knew existed, as a result of going to college, talking to a friend, or sitting in on a guest lecture. Happenstance theory suggests that we should take an active role in seeking out learning experiences and capitalizing on unplanned events and opportunities.

Career Construction Theory

The *career construction theory of vocational development and career counseling*, developed by Mark L. Savickas and others, says that individuals build their careers by imposing meaning on vocational behavior.[4] Career construction theory helps people find work that is meaningful in their lives, rather than trying to fit themselves to jobs. Career construction theory has become relevant in today's uncertain economic times, where stable and predictable career paths no longer exist. A career counseling approach that has gained popularity is the narrative approach that focuses on the individual's understanding of the forces that have shaped their lives. This approach is particularly helpful with multicultural concerns that have been difficult to address in more traditional models. Life themes, social influences, and the process of shaping or constructing one's life story are key components in narrative approaches. The process of being the author of one's life story includes work and live outside or work, as well as multiple life roles such as family member, student, and community member.[5]

Chaos Theory of Careers

The *chaos theory of careers (CTC)* has its roots in general systems theories arising out of math and science. The concept of career is framed at the outset as a system with multiple influences where change is continual. CTC is comprised of three C's—*complexity, chance*, and *change*—as overlapping elements that describe the situational factors, unplanned events, and continual changes in career development. *Complexity* describes all the situational factors that will influence and alter an individual's career plans. Rather than focusing exclusively on values, interests, personality, and skills, CTC recognizes the vast number of contextual influences at play in career development and decision-making. As illustrated with happenstance, *chance* is an important aspect in any career development model. Embracing chance and actively seeking out new opportunities enables more open systems thinking. *Change* is one of the characteristics that makes CTC unique and purely modern; change is fundamental to careers, as interests, values, and any number of other factors will change over time.[6]

Hope-Centered Model of Career Development

Believing that you can make good career decisions and reach your career goals is a very important part of the career development process. Psychologists call this belief in your ability to do something "self-efficacy." The degree to which you believe you can accomplish something, like reaching your career goals, plays a huge role in how you approach planning your career. If you don't believe that you will be able to reach your career goals, you might say, "What's the point? Why should I go to college? I'll never make it anyway." But if you *do* believe that you can accomplish your career goals, your whole attitude will be more positive and purposeful; you'll get a tutor to help you get through a rough course, or you'll work nights just to be able to pay for grad school.

Being hopeful colors the way that you perceive the career development process, right down to how you go about choosing a major. Dr. Spencer Niles and his colleagues Norman Amundson and Hyung Joon Yoon believe so strongly in the power of hope that they developed the *hope-centered model of career development.*[7] In their model of career development, hope is more than just having a positive attitude and is referred to as "action-oriented hope." Hope involves setting goals, developing an action plan to reach those goals, implementing those plans for goal achievement, and being able to adapt and respond to changing conditions. Without hope, we would be unlikely to be motivated enough to engage in career planning activities.

Where to Begin

If you are very confused or undecided about choosing a major, you may want to start by taking an interest inventory. Although interest inventories are often referred to as "career tests," they are not really *tests* because there are no right or wrong answers. Interest inventories identify possible career options based on your interests, values, and personality type.

The *Self-Directed Search* (SDS) was developed by John Holland and is a quick and reliable assessment that can be taken in a pencil-and-paper format or online. Other popular standardized interest inventories are the *Campbell Interest and Skill Survey* and the *Strong Interest Inventory*. Another instrument that is often used in career counseling is the *Myers-Briggs Type Inventory* (MBTI). The MBTI is not an interest inventory—it is a personality assessment. Based on the famous Swiss psychiatrist Carl Jung's theory of psychological types, the MBTI indicates a person's preference for gathering information and making decisions. The results can then be used to help people find work that is meaningful and at which they can be productive. The MBTI is surprisingly insightful in helping people identify career options, especially when combined with an interest inventory like the *Strong Interest Inventory*. If you think an interest inventory would be helpful, make an appointment to take one at your school's career center.

A Four-Step Career Decision-Making Model

There are many theories of career development both in the literature and in practical use, but none claim to hold a "crystal ball," despite how desperately we hope for one. Given the complexity of individuals and fluctuations in the economy, how can we make the best decision about a work future many years from now?

Most career counselors begin working with students using some version of the following four-step approach to career planning:

Step 1—Know Yourself. What are you good at? What do you enjoy doing? Where do you like to work? What's your style? What's important to you? What motivates you? Choose a couple of careers or majors based on what you have learned about yourself.

Step 2—Gather Information. Research each career option that you have chosen. Use the Internet, social media, and your career center to research possible careers to determine the facts about job duties, academic requirements, and employment outlook. If you know that you would like to do something in the business area, for example, research all of the careers that fall within the field of business (e.g., management, purchasing, finance, economics, marketing, logistics, accounting, real estate, and sales).

Step 3—Make Choices. From your research, you should be able to eliminate all but a couple of individual majors or careers. Now you're ready to make some preliminary choices.

Step 4—Try It Out. Take courses in your intended major; do a job shadow, internship, service learning project, or summer job; or volunteer in your intended major. Then reflect on your experience and reevaluate your decision or refine your choices until you find the major that's right for you. Repeat steps 1–4 again as necessary.

(Note: Step 1 will be discussed further in Chapter 4: Who Are You?; step 2 will be covered in Chapter 11: Gathering Data for Good Decision-Making; and steps 3 and 4 will be discussed in Chapter 13: Making Big Career Decisions.)

Be Willing to Explore

Even though we're asked to decide rather early what we want to do with the rest of our lives, we can only begin the process with who we are at this point in time. You may not even realize the full extent of your abilities yet. Some people have talents that, for one reason or other, surface only later in life. Maybe you never knew you could write poetry. You may not have had the opportunity or a reason to try. Then one day an event like 9/11 happens that touches your emotional core in such a way that you begin to express yourself through writing poetry, and a career in creative writing begins to emerge. The adage "You won't know until you try" is true when it comes to choosing a career.

Just as you used your interests and activities in high school to help you pick a college, use your college resources and activities to choose a major. Talk to faculty in an academic department of interest and look at graduation requirements (typically available on a college's website) to find out what kinds of classes your major will entail. Take an intro marketing class and find out more about the major before you make a decision. If you hate the classes or find yourself constantly struggling with them, that's a clue to consider another option. But if you like what you're learning in that class, then take another. Exploring a variety of classes will also help you to identify other previously unexplored interests.

It's helpful to realize that many occupations and jobs share the same core skills and values. For example, if you're not able to pursue the rigorous path of becoming a neurosurgeon, but your core interests and values are medicine and helping others, there are plenty of other related healthcare careers such as nursing, radiology, and medical technology that would be equally satisfying. Or you could become a medical counselor or social worker or another health professional who works with or for the neurosurgeon.

The key is to be able to identify those particular aspects of a profession that interest you. Once you've identified those key factors you might find they are common to several different professions. Now you've broadened your career options and avoided the common pitfall of being locked into only one career option.

Jim

Jim was an incoming freshman who was referred to career services by his academic advisor. He had already gone through the freshman orientation program and had registered for his core courses. However, his counselor suggested that he work with a career counselor regarding a career direction. Jim's results on the *Strong Interest Inventory* revealed interests in conventional occupations like accounting and investigative occupations like biology and health science. Jim played sports in high school and at one time considered kinesiology and athletic training. After we had discussed career options in the hard sciences and health care, Jim said that he might be interested in EMT.

Jim also had a strong interest in accounting. He said he took accounting classes in high school and really enjoyed them. Jim said that the reason choosing a major was so difficult was that he had such divergent interests. And he was right. The requirements for accounting are vastly different from the requirements for kinesiology.

Over subsequent visits, Jim thoroughly researched each career of interest, including watching videos that illustrated what a person in that career did on a daily basis. When he still couldn't decide between accounting and athletic training, I suggested that he try taking introductory courses in each major. After taking an accounting course, Jim realized that it was different than the course he had in high school and didn't hold the same interest for him anymore. Jim eventually opted to major in athletic training and pick up his EMT certification on the side.

If You're in High School

If you're still in high school, begin with your interests. Think about what you like to do—in class, after school, and at home. What are your favorite classes? What is your least favorite? Which subjects seem to come easily to you? What do you like to do outside of class? What types of books, movies, and videos do you enjoy? What are your hobbies? Can you identify any common themes that can lead to a career?

Most high school students have not accumulated enough work experience to be able to identify work values and attitudes. And you may have only been exposed to a small number of careers in school or through the people you know. Look around and take note of all of the different jobs in the world. Careers are everywhere—from the bus driver to your guidance counselor or football coach, to your family doctor or dentist, to the retail clerk in the department store. Talk to employed adults and ask them about their occupations. Ask your teachers, your neighbors, and your family members for input about their careers. What do they like and dislike about their occupations?

Begin thinking about what kind of job you would like to have. If you already have a part-time or summer job, then you are already gathering information about that type of job (and whether or not you want to do it for a living). If you are not working, consider volunteering or getting a part-time job to learn more about work and in which employment settings you might enjoy. My first summer job was at a pick-your-own strawberry farm. We didn't pick the strawberries, but we directed customers and checked them out when they finished picking. Although I didn't necessarily enjoy the customer service aspect of the job, I learned some valuable work-related skills such as how to work collaboratively with my coworkers and how to successfully interact with the public.

CHAPTER THREE

Dispelling Common Career Myths

Myths are public dreams, dreams are private myths.

—Joseph Campbell

Many of us have heard stories about people who picked the wrong major or found themselves in careers they later did not enjoy. Most college students choose a career field based on a handful of familiar options. Business is still the most common major among college students. According to the National Center for Education Statistics, the top five most popular college degrees awarded in 2013–2014 are business administration, liberal arts, nursing, psychology, and general studies.[1]

When asked why they chose their major, the answers that most students give sound something like this: "I chose engineering because my father is an engineer," or "Technology is the way to go these days," or "I'll be able to find a good paying job if I become a nurse."

Why We Make Poor Career Choices

In my experience, the two most common reasons for poor career choice is the lack of sound career information and lack of self-knowledge. Here are some common examples of why students make poor career choices:

1. **Not understanding who you are and where your strengths lie.** Perhaps the most difficult situation is when there is a disconnect between what students want to do and where their strengths lie. When I was in high school, several

of us wanted to become veterinarians after reading James Herriot's best seller *All Creatures Great and Small.* The problem was that some of us didn't have the academic strengths to be successful in that major: get through the biology, chemistry, and calculus courses *and* maintain the 4.0 GPA required to get into vet school. The trick is to find a career that best fits who you are—based on your interests, strengths, personality, and work style. And the only way to discover that is to do some serious reflection and research.

2. **Majoring in something for the wrong reasons.** We hear a lot about the importance of "finding your passion" or finding your "bliss" in the popular media and literature. The theory that following your passion leads to success first surfaced in the 1970s. While it's certainly important to find an occupation that you enjoy doing, turning your passion into a job isn't always the best answer because passion is based on emotion, not on fact. It's like being madly in love with someone and then finding out after you're married that you are incompatible. You didn't see their flaws or, if you did, ignored them. Think about how many wannabe lead guitar players are out there who are unemployed. Just because you're passionate about something doesn't mean that you're going to be able to get a job doing that.

3. **Taking the easy route.** Students do themselves a great injustice by taking "the easy route" in college. Nothing in life that is worthwhile is ever easy. Pursuing an easy major that you don't necessarily like or discounting a major that you do like because it requires graduate or professional school is not good career planning. Think of going to college as a way to invest in your future and in your future success and happiness. *Minimum effort will land you a minimum wage job.*

4. **Going for the money.** Choosing an occupation simply because of the salary doesn't take into account whether you're suited for the profession or whether you'll like the work. Many students at my community college choose nursing because it offers the guarantee of a good job at a high salary after only two years (two-year accredited RN program). The $27 or $28 an hour starting salary may sound great, but nursing is also academically challenging and not everyone has the stomach to take care of sick people.

5. **Being overly influenced by others.** Students receive advice from many people, including their families, about what they *should* do with their lives before they have had a chance to make that decision for themselves. The more your career choice is based on other people's preferences (parent, friend, or spouse), the more likely it is to be a good choice for *them*, but not for you. You're the one who will have to live with your career choice for 8 hours a day, 52 weeks in the year. Go ahead and ask people for ideas and impressions, but then make up your own mind.

6. **Discounting a career because of misinformation.** Be aware of stereotypes or biases based on incomplete or faulty information about careers (e.g., teachers don't make very much money; retail jobs are about folding sweaters at the

GAP). Another reason students choose inappropriate majors is that they are overly influenced by what they see on television. When popular forensic shows like *CSI* first came out, many students wanted to major in forensic science until they learned how many chemistry courses were required. Sometimes we tend to be so swept away by the fame, prestige, or romance of high-profile professions that we forget to look at *all* of the aspects of that career. No matter how glamorous a job appears, there are always negative aspects. Usually, a high level of profile or fame is accompanied by an equally high level of stress, pressure, and demand on one's personal time and the very public consequences of making a mistake. In the case of the ER surgeon, you may only be seeing what television wants you to see—fame, wealth, respect, or the drama surrounding saving a life. But what you don't see (and what you would have to live with every day) are the long, grueling hours; the hospital bureaucracy; moments of extreme stress; threats of a lawsuit; and the possibility of losing a patient. So know who you are and what you can and cannot handle and be aware of the reasons behind the choices you make.

Another common misconception is that everyone should get a four-year degree, but there are a number of occupations at the two-year degree level that make more money than many bachelor's degrees. There are plenty of opportunities in the skilled trades (HVAC, automotive, welding, construction, and diesel mechanics) and engineering technologies. Many people discount the skilled trades because they think that they're going to get their hands dirty. Technological advances and computer applications have transformed many of the skilled trades into relatively clean working conditions that require workers to use both their brains *and* their hands.

Common Career Myths

Contrary to popular belief, career development does not stop once you graduate from college—it continues throughout your life. From your first job to the next one until you finally decide to retire, you will continue to evaluate and readjust your career goals. You may change jobs or even careers, go back to school, or decide to start your own business. Think of your college degree as the beginning foundation of your career. As you go through life, you will constantly be adding to that foundation with life and work experiences, new positions and employers, and continued educational experiences.

Most people think they know everything about choosing a career. If you are one of those people, you may be surprised to know that what many people believe about choosing a career is actually a myth—and, as a result, the reason they end up choosing an unsatisfying career. If you really want to find a fulfilling career, then you should know the facts about how to choose one. I've listed 10 of the most common career myths and have dispelled them with a healthy dose of "career reality."

Myth 1—Most Students Who Enter College Are Certain of Their Major

Fact: This is the most common fallacy among college students. Although statistics vary, at least 50 percent of entering college students are undecided about their majors.[2] If you are uncertain about your major, you are not alone, even though you may think, "all of my friends know exactly what they want to be when they graduate."

Myth 2—Once a Student Declares a Major, He or She Will Stick with It

Fact: Although many students enter college fully committed to their major, the fact is that 80 percent of students change their majors at least once and, on average, college students will change their majors three or more times before they graduate.[3]

Myth 3—Students Should Choose a Major Based on the Current Job Market

Fact: The problem with choosing a major based on current job hiring is that the job market constantly fluctuates. Employment opportunities are essentially a function of the basic economic principles of *supply* and *demand*. If there are only a few graduates in a particular major, then market demand will outstrip supply and result in an increase in salary and benefits in that job as employers compete for a limited supply of qualified candidates. However, if thousands of college students choose that major because of the number of job openings, they may find that eventually the job market will become flooded because supply now exceeds the demand. A change in supply and demand can happen in any occupation. Some occupations are more sensitive to changes in economic conditions and technological advances than others. Nonetheless, it is wise to try to choose a major with a reasonable employment outlook. Job outlook trends can be useful information if used judiciously and not as the only factor in your career decision-making process.

Myth 4—There Is One Perfect Career for Me

Fact: Finding the "perfect" career is a myth because there is usually something negative about every career or job. Although there may not be one "perfect" career for you, the fact is that there may be several "right" career choices. If you think that nursing is your perfect calling, for example, ask yourself what it is about nursing that really appeals to you. If your answer is that nursing will allow you to care for people, then you may be just as happy working as a social worker, a physical therapist, a home health aide, a minister, or the director of a women's shelter. Once you've identified your core interests and life values, you will be able to broaden your career options and avoid the trap of being locked into only one career choice.

Myth 5—My Major Is Going to Lead to My Career

Fact: Most employers care more about the knowledge and skills that you have obtained than they do about your major. Unless you are planning to enter a field that requires specific technical skills or a professional certification (e.g., engineering, accounting, education), there is a great deal of flexibility in the type of major that you choose. There are usually several majors that can lead to a particular job or career, and vice versa.

Myth 6—Once a Student Commits to a Major, He or She Will Be Stuck in That Career for the Rest of His or Her Life

Fact: Career planning is an ongoing process. In our current economy, no one will stay in the same job for his or her entire lifetime, even if that's what he or she truly wants. Ninety-one percent of millennials expect to stay in a job for less than three years, according to the Future Workplace "Multiple Generations at Work" survey.[4] Today, the typical person entering the workforce can expect to work for an average of 10 employers before age 40 and hold 12–15 jobs by the time he or she retires.[5] What this data shows is that your major will not lock you into a specific career. There will be plenty of opportunities to change your major or your job. Your goal should be to make the best choice that you can, at this point in time, and then evaluate and reevaluate your choice as you move forward in your career.

Myth 7—Liberal Arts, Arts, and Humanities Majors Are Usually Unemployable after College

Fact: The skills that students learn in a liberal arts education are ones sought after by many employers: interpersonal communication, writing, research, and critical thinking. These are called transferable skills—skills learned in one area that can be used in a variety of other areas. Liberal arts, arts, and humanities majors are employed in a wide range of careers, even though the job title may not have an obvious correlation to the name of their major.

Myth 8—If I Wait Long Enough, I'll Eventually End Up in the Right Career

Fact: Most people will benefit from fully investigating and considering different occupations. It is unlikely that you will just land into the occupation that best fits your interests, skills, and values. Where luck does play a role is when you are open to exploring new possibilities by trying new classes; talking to people about their careers; and doing internships, volunteer work, or part-time jobs. By actively exploring career options, you may discover a major that you hadn't been aware of before. Take charge of your career path instead of leaving it up to chance.

Myth 9—Career Assessments Will Tell Me Exactly What Career Is Right for Me

Fact: Assessments are one part of the career planning process and can provide you with additional information about yourself that will help you identify some appropriate options based on your interests, abilities, values, and personality style. No test, however, can tell you what to do with your life or predict the "perfect" career. You will receive the most value from an assessment when you discuss the results with a trained career counselor or coach who knows how to interpret the results.

Myth 10—I Should Choose an Occupation Based on My Strongest Skills

Fact: Good career choices are based on several factors. Although abilities are an important consideration, abilities are only one of the components of career decision-making. What you enjoy doing and what is important to you should also be taken into consideration. Just because you are good at something doesn't mean that you'll enjoy doing it for a living.

Nicole

Nicole was a bright, articulate sophomore who was undecided about her major. She had several interests ranging from math to theater. She was good at math, definitely a people person, and loved theater and photography. Her mother suggested actuarial science but Nicole thought it would be too boring. When asked why she thought it was so difficult to choose a major she said that it was hard for her to put herself into one job for the rest of her life. She didn't want to be "stuck" in a job that she didn't like just to earn money. I suggested that she view the situation as just a starting point. There was no reason to think that she'd be stuck—there would be lots of opportunities to change direction, go back to school, or learn something new. No one stays in one job forever anymore. Visibly relieved, Nicole and I discussed each of her options. By the end of our meeting she was able to narrow down her list of possibilities (counseling, education, actuary, marketing, occupational therapy, and physical therapy) to two areas, marketing and occupational therapy.

CHAPTER FOUR

Who Are You?

An unexamined life is not worth living.

—Socrates

The first step in choosing the right career is to know yourself—your interests, values, motivations, tendencies, and personality. If you do not know what you're good at or what you'd like to do on a daily basis, then it will be almost impossible to find a suitable career. Use your interests and natural abilities as a guide to find a good match between yourself and a potential career. Find something that you can be good at *and* enjoy.

Interests + Abilities + Values + Personality = A Career with Meaning and Purpose

Sonja Lyubomirsky, a psychology professor at the University of California, Riverside and author of the best seller *The How of Happiness: A Scientific Approach to Getting the Life You Want*, has done extensive research on positive psychology and happiness. Her research shows that 50 percent of our happiness is determined by genetics, 10 percent by life circumstances, and 40 percent by our own thoughts and actions.[1] Bringing this into a career development context, you are responsible for a large part of your own happiness through the activities you choose to do, the choices you make, and the goals you set. If you want to have a more meaningful and purposeful life, then you should try to make career choices that fit your interests, strengths, and core values.

Interests

Undecided students are often so overwhelmed with the entire process of choosing a major or career that they just aren't sure how to get started.

That's why most career professionals begin by asking you to identify your interests.

Interests are a logical first place to start in the career decision-making process. Why? Because for most people, it's important to enjoy what you're going to do every day for the next 40+ years of your working life.

Interests are things and activities that you like to do. Everyone's interests are a little bit different. Some people really enjoy computing mathematical formulas, and others, not so much. When you are excited about something, chances are that those activities are the things you like best. Most people also do well at the activities they really enjoy. With enough investigation and planning, you can find work that excites and energizes you. When you are paid to do a job that you love, it may not even feel like "work."

If you're having trouble coming up with things that you like to do, try a fun activity like asking yourself the following questions:

a. The hours seem to fly by when I _____.
b. I often lose track of time when I _____.
c. I am happiest when I _____.
d. I could _____ all day long.
e. If I had a zillion dollars, I would _____.

It will come as no surprise that finding work that you enjoy is a very important part of the career decision-making process. If you don't like what you do on a daily basis, your day can become very long indeed. I can speak quite knowledgeably about this—I've had a lot of jobs that I didn't like. In fact, over the course of my working life I can name three jobs (current job included) that I actually enjoyed.

> The road to happiness lies in two simple principles: Find what it is that interests you and that you can do well. And when you find it, put your whole soul into it—every bit of energy and ambition and natural ability you have.
>
> —John D. Rockefeller III

Abilities

Abilities (what am I good at and what skills or talents do I possess) are important in helping you *reach* your career goal. Abilities are your areas of strength. If the ability seems to come naturally, then they are referred to as "talents." When abilities are used in the workplace, they are referred to as "skills."

Most people enjoy doing what they do well. However, sometimes our interests are not aligned with our strengths. You need to be objective about your abilities and fully understand the requirements of the career you want to pursue. Many students begin college in academically challenging majors like premed or engineering with high hopes and aspirations. Then they fail their first calculus or chemistry exam and their second one, and eventually come to the painful realization that they may have to modify their career goals and find another direction. This experience can be extremely traumatic. For this reason, it's wise to take the time to understand the requirements of your major thoroughly and compare them against your strengths and weaknesses. Your goal should be to put yourself in a position where you are going to succeed. If you decide to pursue a rigorous academic major, go ahead and give it your best shot—but have a backup plan, just in case.

Values

Our values determine what is important to us. In the workplace, our values will determine whether or not a job will be satisfying. Some values are "intrinsic," meaning that they offer intangible rewards—those related to motivation and satisfaction at work on a daily basis. Other values are 'extrinsic," the tangible rewards or conditions you find at work, including the physical setting, job titles, benefits, and earning potential.

Again, everyone is different. Some people value responsibility or independence, while others value prestige or status. Depending on your personal values (also called core values), you may want to work for a company that offers rapid promotion or would like to work in a setting where you are your own boss. Work values have to do with the reasons people receive satisfaction from their jobs. If your values are expressed in your work, then your job takes on meaning and purpose. If your work does not provide personal satisfaction, then it becomes meaningless and boring. If you have the interest and ability to be a physician, for example, you may feel compelled to use those skills to help children in the inner city or in third world countries where good health care is rare. This altruistic part of the job is called a *value*, and will eventually make a difference in what type of job you choose within a field, and how happy you will be as a result.

As you move through life, your values may change. For example, when you start your career, you may value money and status. But after you have a family, you may begin to place more value on work-life balance.

Some values are more closely associated with a particular occupation than others. An occupation that allows you to use your physical ability, like joining the Navy Seals or becoming a rock climber, would be suitable for someone who valued physical fitness and challenge. Justice and social consciousness might be important values to someone in the legal profession, whereas helping others or making a difference might be important values for someone in social work or a counseling profession. Being able to identify and prioritize your work values will help you make a better choice of work environments and increase the likelihood that you will find a career that makes getting up in the morning to go to work a pleasure. When your work and your nonwork lives are aligned with your core values, you will feel most fully alive and energized.

Here are the definitions of 25 common work values. Identify which values are important to you:

1. **Help people.** Working with or helping people; having compassion and respect for others; developing meaningful relationships with others; helping make the world a better place to live.

   Careers that involve this value are nursing; health-care professions; education; counseling or psychology; social work human services; customer service; and service organizations like nonprofit groups that focus on human, civil, or political rights.

2. **Productivity.** Being results oriented; seeing projects come to completion; being able to check off the "to-do" list; enjoys a fast-paced work environment.

   Careers in manufacturing, engineering, and working in any fast-paced office environment would fit this value.

3. **Independence or autonomy.** The ability to do your own thing; working alone or unsupervised; being in charge of your own schedule; may prefer a flexible work schedule.

   Professional careers, careers in art, and entrepreneurship usually offer more autonomy.

4. **Stability and security.** A guaranteed annual salary in a permanent position with a secure and stable company; little chance of being outsourced; supervisory assistance; predictable job duties.

   Consider career fields that are in high demand, like accounting, computer science, and health care. Jobs within the state and federal government are considered to be stable and secure.

5. **Prestige.** Recognition among peers; status; respect.

   Typical careers might be physician, attorney, and politician, but this value can be associated with a high level of expertise in any profession.

6. **Intellectually challenging or stimulating.** Requires research, thinking, and problem-solving; requires the ability to deal with new ideas; work with creative and intellectually stimulating people.

   In the general, this value is often found in research, science, and higher education.

7. **Adventure.** Excitement; physical or mental risk-taking; ability to travel; requires excellent physical health.

   Careers that require special experience or training such as protective services, first responders, wilderness guide, skydiving instructor, ski instructor, test pilot, and so on.

8. **Financial rewards.** Effort is rewarded with a high salary, bonuses, and other compensations; the ability to own nice things.

   This value is often associated with commission-based work. Typical occupations that provide higher incomes early in your career are sales, finance, and computer software development.

9. **Creativity.** The ability to work spontaneously; nonroutine; free to develop new ideas or designs; work with abstract ideas and concepts; work in teams of people developing new products or ways of doing things.

   Fields linked most closely with this value are teaching, advertising, art, fashion design, graphic design, marketing, engineering design, public relations, and freelance writing or journalism.

10. **Leadership.** Being in charge; ability to influence people and opinions; making decisions and supervising others; possessing power, authority, and control.

    Typical career areas might be found in politics, academia, law, and business management.

11. **Relationships.** Organizational affiliation; prefer a harmonious work environment; values friendships at work; public contact.

    Any occupation involving helping or caring for people (e.g., teaching, counseling, health care) would embrace this value including some customer service positions.

12. **Variety.** Dislikes routine; stimulated by multitasking or being involved in different types of tasks; may prefer a fast-paced environment.

    This value is often associated with jobs in which people assume several work roles (e.g., nonprofit, small businesses), jobs that involve travel, and jobs that involve moving around the company or travel between locations.

Health care, reception, marketing, sales, retail, and any job that deals with a high volume of customers would contain variety.

13. **Physical activity**. Actively using your body or muscles; working outdoors; requires a level of physical fitness.

    Careers that fall under this category include health education, exercise science, athletic trainer, military, nurse, firefighter, landscaper, organic farmer, wildlife biologist, marine scientist, archeologist, construction, masonry, electrician, mountain guide, forest ranger, wildlife biologist, organic farmer, skydiving instructor, conservationist, coast guard, paramedic/EMT, ski instructor, geologist, photographer, journalist, botanist, gardener, landscaper, civil engineer, and large animal veterinarian.

14. **Advancement**. Ability to work your way up in a company; quality and productivity are rewarded; opportunity to attain goals, money, better lifestyle, and so on.

    Sales, marketing, finance, business, and entrepreneurship are often associated with this value.

15. **Accuracy**. Being exact or correct; may prefer an orderly work environment.

    Careers that value accuracy include accounting, auditing, medical billing and coding, secretarial support, and any career involving mathematics.

16. **Ethics**. Conducting oneself in an honest and fair manner; doing what's right; adhering to ethical standards.

    This value can apply to any career or employer. May have a preference for faith-based organizations or companies.

17. **Beauty**. Appreciates physical, visual, or aesthetic beauty in all forms.

    Careers that value beauty are found in the fine arts, photography, artistic or historic preservation, the fashion industry, the health and beauty industry, modeling, makeup artist, fitness trainer, cosmetologist, retail, and so on.

18. **Justice/social justice**. Rules are applied fairly in society; individuals are protected and basic rights are upheld. Individuals are treated equitably and with respect and have access to all opportunities in society regardless of gender, sexuality, religion, political affiliations, age, race, belief, disability, location, social class, or socioeconomic status).

    Law enforcement, law, criminal justice, social services professions, education, health care, counseling, social work, victim advocacy, and specific nonprofit and lobbyist positions all value social justice.

19. **Health/wellness**. Important to be physically healthy; maintain a healthy lifestyle through good eating habits, exercise, and healthy living habits.

    Careers aligned with this value are holistic medicine, nutrition, physical education, and health and wellness education.

20. **Power**. Exercising control, influence, or authority over oneself or others.

    Leadership roles in any occupation would qualify. Occupations such as finance, law, and business management.

21. **Recognition**. Receiving attention, accolades, or awards; recognition from peers.

    This value can be found in higher education, research, business, politics, or any position in which you are noticed and appreciated for the work you do on a daily basis.

22. **Responsibility**. Being reliable; keeping your word; completing what is expected of you.

    This value can apply to any job or profession.

23. **Respect**. Being treated in a respectful manner by others.

    Although this value can apply to any occupation, most are prevalent in leadership positions or occupations where a professional has gained a high level of expertise.

24. **Travel**. Seeing and experiencing different places; not staying in the same place all of the time; may involve learning about and appreciating other cultures.

    When applied to the work setting, this is a desire to work for a company in which you can physically travel or visit clients/companies located in another part of the country or overseas. Typical careers include business, hospitality, and the military.

25. **Competition**. Comparing self to others; striving to be the best that you can be.

    Careers that value competition include sales, business, sports, and marketing.

Steven

Steven entered college as a business major. In high school he was good at math and very active in sports. After completing two accounting courses he realized that he wasn't interested in his courses. Worried that he was in the wrong major, he came to the career center for help. Steve's interests, and his abilities, seemed to fall into three categories: math, science (biology), and sports. When asked what he did outside of school, Steve talked about enjoying outdoor activities with his father like hunting, fishing, and hiking the Appalachian Trail.

> I took Business and Accounting courses because everyone says those are good majors to go into, but I just couldn't see myself sitting behind a desk all day. I'm more of an outdoors person like my father.

Although he didn't know it at the time, Steve was describing his values and his preferred work environment. After researching careers that involved math, science, and work environments that allowed him to be outdoors, Steve was really drawn to the field of environmental science and began taking courses in that major. He later transferred to a four-year school in the state that was well known for environmental geology. Steve also added a minor in environmental education so he could share his passion for the outdoors with others.

As you go through the process of identifying your personal values, make sure that your values are truly your own. If you feel like you *should* do something, then stop for a moment and try to figure out where that is coming from. The chances are that it's coming from someone else—your parents, your family members, friends, etc. Your personal values are a central part of who you are—and who you want to be. Being aware of your core values can also help you identify when something is missing in your life. Don't fall into the trap of trying to make your work supplement something that is missing from your life. Get back in touch with your core values. By becoming more aware of the role of your values in your life, you can use them as a guide to make the best choice in any situation.

Personality Style

Are you someone who thrives in a fast-paced, busy environment, or do you work better when you have time to reflect before making decisions? Do you prefer working alone, or are you more productive when you can brainstorm ideas with a group of people? Are you an optimist or a pessimist? Do you have a tendency to rush in and take charge, or would you rather patiently listen to what others think and then decide as a group as to how to proceed? Each of us has a unique personality that differentiates us from other people. Our personality style determines how we are likely to act and feel in a variety of situations. Personality style also comes into play when choosing a career. Remember that you will be spending almost a third of your life working. That can be a *very* long time if you don't enjoy your job or your career. If you're unhappy at work, it can also affect your happiness at home, so it's important to get it right.

Certain careers are inherently better suited for particular personality types. Think about Holland's six types—a creative, expressive personality type (A) will feel stifled in a routine, detail-ordered work environment (C). But having said that, it doesn't mean that a social type of individual can't be happy working in a conventional career because you can always select a work environment that best matches your personality style. Let's look at accounting, for example. If you enjoy accounting but need to have daily social contact, then you would be happier as a CPA in private practice where you see lots of clients or as someone who teaches accounting in high school or college. On the other hand, if you prefer a quiet environment where you can do your own work undisturbed, with a minimum of distractions and less people contact, then a position as a controller or auditor may be a better choice for you.

Your personality style, not unlike your values, becomes more important when you begin working and may play a role in determining how happy or successful you will be at your job. Your unique personality style should play a major role when it comes to selecting the right career.

Two of the most commonly talked about personality styles are extraversion and introversion. Which style do you prefer?

Outgoing or Extraverted Personality:

- You get your energy from outside activities, people, and events.
- You love to talk to people and enjoy working in groups.
- You can assimilate an onslaught of stimulation but don't like to get bogged down in paperwork or details.
- You like to jump into action and make things happen.
- You seek variety and interaction and like to express emotion.
- You are energized by being around people.
- You tend to act before you think.
- You've been called ambitious, motivated, and driven.

Introverted Personality:

- You get your energy from ideas, memories, and "alone time."
- You work best on your own and always hated those group projects assigned in school.
- You're fairly quiet and prefer to follow a routine.
- You think deeply about things.
- You're usually adverse to change but are a dependable worker.
- You tend to think before you act.
- Being around too many people for too long drains you.
- You like to know a few people well.
- You like to work alone and need a quiet environment for concentration.

If you prefer to work independently with minimal outside distractions, Table 4.1 provides a list of 26 great careers for you.

It's important to note that introversion and extraversion exist on a spectrum. Some introverts may be "more introverted" than others and thus require more time alone to recharge their batteries, and some extraverts might need more stimulation than others.[2] In the general population there is approximately a 50/50 split between introverts and extraverts.

Table 4.2 provides a list of typical college majors arranged by Holland personality type.

Table 4.1   26 Great Careers for Introverts

1. Social media manager	14. Carpenter
2. Actuary	15. Small engine mechanic
3. Electrician	16. Forester
4. Paralegal	17. Museum curator
5. Medical records technician	18. Librarian
6. Graphic designer	19. Fine artist
7. Technical writer	20. Video game designer
8. Accountant	21. Writer
9. Computer programmer	22. Private chef
10. Truck driver	23. Statistician
11. Lab technician	24. Animal breeder/trainer
12. Market research analyst	25. Court reporter
13. Translator	26. Astronomer

Table 4.2   College Majors by Holland Personality Type

Realistic	Investigative	Artistic
Agriculture/forestry	Animal science	Advertising
Animal science	Anthropology	Architecture
Architectural engineering tech	Astronomy	Art history
Automotive	Biochemistry	Art education
Building construction	Biological sciences	Classics
Computer-aided drafting and design	Chemistry	Communications
Criminal justice	Computer science	English

(Continued)

Realistic	Investigative	Artistic
Dental assisting/hygiene	Engineering	Foreign language
Electronic engineering tech	Forestry	Graphic design
Engineering	Geography	History
Environmental studies	Geology	Interior design
Exercise science	Mathematics	Journalism
Geology	Medical technology	Music
Health and physical education	Medicine	Music education
Horticulture	Nursing	Speech/drama
Medical technology	Nutrition	
Nuclear engineering	Pharmacy	
Plumbing/heating	Philosophy	
Radiological technology	Physical therapy	
Recreation/tourism management	Physics	
Respiratory therapy	Psychology	
Sport management	Sociology	
Surgical tech	Statistics	

Social	Enterprising	Conventional
Audiology	Advertising	Accounting
Counseling	Agricultural economics	Business
Criminal justice	Broadcasting	Computer science
Elementary education	Communications	Economics
History	Economics	Finance
Human development	Finance	Mathematics
Human services	Industrial relations	Medical office
Library science	Insurance	Medical billing and coding
Occupational therapy	Journalism	Statistics
Nursing	Law	
Nutrition	Management	
Psychology	Marketing	
Social work	Political science	
Special education	Public administration	
	Speech	

Assessment Tests

There are a multitude of career and personality assessments that measure everything from intelligence to personal compatibility. You might have an idea of what you're good at, but do you really know all your skills, personality, strengths, and most importantly your values? Knowing how to verbalize what you're good at and what's important is beneficial not only in choosing a career, writing a resume, and interviewing for a job after graduation. Take the time to figure this out. If you are unsure about your career direction or are feeling very overwhelmed, it is helpful to start with an interest inventory such as the *Self-Directed Search* or the *Strong Interest Inventory*, followed by a personality assessment like the *Myers-Briggs Type Indicator*, an ability assessment like the *Ability Explorer*, or a strengths assessment such as *StrengthsFinder*. Your college career center can help you choose the assessment(s) that is best for you. Although there are a number of "free" questionnaires and surveys available on the Internet, you'll get more benefit from using an industry-standard instrument interpreted by a trained career professional. Most college career centers offer career assessments free of charge or for a nominal fee.

Understanding all of the factors that make you unique will help you select a career that matches your talents, skills, interests, personality style, and circumstances. If you're not sure what major or career you might be interested in, then begin with an interest inventory. Work with a career counselor to gather about yourself and create an accurate picture of who you are.

Journey Back to the Past

Sometimes reflecting back to our childhood can give us a more unbiased picture of who we are and where our core interests lie. As we grow older, many of us have been taught to suppress what we want or like to please others. But to obtain true career happiness, you must know what you truly want to do, not just what others would like you to do.

To help you get back in touch with your core interests, try to answer the following questions as thoroughly and thoughtfully as you can. See if there are any trends or common themes that can be used to point you toward a possible career. When researching careers or occupations, keep these answers in mind and make some mental comparisons to the jobs or careers you are investigating.

1. When you were a child, what did you want to be when you grew up? Why?
2. What did you do for fun? What were your hobbies? Do you still do any of these things today? Why or why not?

3. Did you prefer to play by yourself, with one or two others, or with a large group of people?

4. What things were important to you then? What made you happy?

5. What subjects did you enjoy in high school? In which subjects did you receive your highest grades?

6. Did you have any special talents (art, music, sports) when you were a child? Are you still pursuing these activities?

7. What extracurricular activities were you involved with in high school? Which did you enjoy most? Why?

8. What was your greatest achievement or accomplishment? How did you go about reaching it? How did you feel afterward? What does this tell you about yourself?

9. What did your parents/guardians do for a living? Your grandparents? Aunts and uncles? Other close relatives? How did this influence you?

10. What person do you admire most? Why? Has anyone influenced your life? How?

11. What are your strongest personal qualities? What do your friends like the most about you?

12. Name the highest point in your life. Why was it so special or important?

CHAPTER FIVE

Careers for Compassionate People

When people believe in themselves, it is amazing what they can accomplish.

—Sam Walton

How Do I Know If I'm a Compassionate Person?

Compassionate people consider themselves, caring, and empathetic and enjoy helping, serving, or caring for others. Most compassionate people dislike working alone and would rather interact with and work cooperatively with other people. They value relationships and see themselves as someone who is helpful, friendly, empathetic, a good listener, and trustworthy.

One of my students came into the office and said to me, "What else can I do if I'm caring and compassionate but don't want to go into nursing?" Compassionate people often choose careers in health care, education, counseling, allied health, medicine, human resources, animals, or personal care. But those aren't the only careers for caring and compassionate people. The traits of being helpful and caring can be incorporated into a variety of careers such as administrative assistant, personal trainer, clergy, funeral director, nutritionist, college student affairs staff, and nonprofit director.

Careers in Education

People who work in education and training occupations have direct contact with individuals in an educational setting. People in these occupations generally have interests in working with people and skills in teaching, tutoring, or instructing. They value helping others learn and develop.

Most career opportunities are found in public and private schools, two-year colleges, four-year colleges, and universities. There are also a variety of opportunities in nonschool settings such as corporate trainers, vocational educators, health educators, recreational leaders, environmental educators, tour guides, and even guide dog trainers. Teachers can also become private tutors or teach private classes, such as private music or voice lessons. Others become textbook editors, educational software developers, employment counselors, or art therapists.

Daycare or learning centers usually prefer teachers and teacher aides who have experience or an associate degree in early childhood education. Employment settings can be found at daycare and learning centers or Head Start.

Public school educators must complete a bachelor's degree in education and obtain the appropriate teaching certificate or license for the subject area and grade level they wish to teach. These requirements will vary by state. Obtaining a dual certification will often increase employability. Private schools and charter schools may not require a traditional teaching certification or licensure, but they will prefer someone with a bachelor's degree in the subject matter that will be taught (e.g., history). Obtain a master's degree in the subject area for increased employability. Employers are public and private elementary, middle, and secondary schools and charter schools.

To become a principal or superintendent, acquire several years of teaching experience and then obtain a certificate in school administration. Earning a PhD in higher education is preferable.

Library services and specialty services such as speech-language pathology, reading specialist, school psychology, and school counseling all require a master's degree.

If you are interested in teaching in higher education (two-year colleges and technical colleges, four-year colleges and universities, medical and professional schools), a master's or PhD degree is required to teach. Earn a PhD in higher education administration for upper-level positions in university administration and to teach at research universities and professional schools.

A master's degree in student personnel, student development, or counseling is generally preferred for student affairs positions at colleges and universities.

There are many employment opportunities for educators in business and industry. Some of these include employment with corporations; consulting firms; textbook, newspaper, magazine, or book publishers; test-preparation companies; education product sales; and staffing agencies. In addition, federal and state government agencies often hire educators. Examples of the employers include the Department of Education, Health and Human

Table 5.1   Jobs in Education

Education

Audiology and speech pathology	Curriculum supervision
Early childhood teacher	Elementary, middle, secondary teacher
Guidance counseling	Library/information services
Principal	School psychologist
School social worker	Special education
Superintendent	

Higher Education

Administration	Library services
Instructional services	Student affairs
Teaching and research	

Adult and Continuing Education

Administration	Community workshops/classes
ESL instructor	Literacy instructor
In-service training and staff development	Veteran's coordinator

Business and Industry

Consulting	Customer service
Human resources	Publishing and technical writing
Sales	Training and development

Government

Administration	Evaluation
Management	Planning
Research and writing	

Nonprofit

Fund raising	Programming
Public relations	Teaching or training
Volunteer coordinator	

Services, Library of Congress, Overseas Schools for Military Dependents, Peace Corps, National Science Foundation, and National Endowment for the Humanities.

To obtain positions at the state or federal level, learn the nuances of federal and state application procedures. Top positions in government usually require extensive experience and an advanced degree.

Nonprofit agencies will also hire individuals with education degrees and backgrounds for positions as volunteer coordinators, event coordinators, and fund-raisers. Examples of potential employers are adoption agencies, Boy or Girl Scouts, Chambers of Commerce, community recreation centers, social services agencies, professional organizations, United Way agencies, and the YMCA/YWCA.

To find employment in the nonprofit sector, it will be helpful to gain experience through volunteer work or internships and to develop your writing and public speaking skills.

Adult education positions can be found in and outside of public education systems. Possible employers include K-12 school systems, colleges and universities, and community organizations such as the Red Cross, hospitals, museums, and professional associations.

To work in a college or university, attain a master's degree or a PhD in adult education. For a nonschool setting, it is helpful to have teaching or instructional experience.

How much does a teacher make? According to Salary.com, the median annual salary for an elementary school teacher is $55,464 and for a high school teacher, $57,832 (Table 5.1).[1]

The average median salary for college professors can range from $64,000 for an assistant professor to over $84,000 for a full professor, depending on the specialty area.[2]

Careers in Health Care

- Do you like to deal with people?
- Are you comfortable with science?
- Are you comfortable in a health-care setting?
- Are you a team player?
- Are you prepared to keep up with developments in your field?

If you answered "yes" to two or more of these questions, then a career in health care may be right for you.

According to Diversity Matters, "One of the first questions you should ask yourself is how much you want to deal with people. For instance, it is important for nurses, pediatricians, and occupational therapists to have a warm and caring personality. By contrast, other health careers such as a clinical laboratory scientist, pathologist, or medical illustrator, involve little or no personal contact with patients."[3]

You do not need to be a medical doctor to have a well-paying career in the health-care field. Health-care careers are expected to continue to boom because the population is aging and living longer, healthier lives. The following are brief definitions of occupations found in the medical field including the amount of training required and average annual salary. See Explore Health Careers at http://www.explorehealthcareers.org for a complete list of health-care occupations and current salary figures.

Allied Health

· **Anesthesiologist**. A specialized physician who administers anesthetics during surgical procedures. Anesthesiologists monitor patients during surgery and recovery and also treat chronic pain. Education: A medical degree, residency, national license, state license, and board certification. Average annual salary: $456,681.[4]

Cardiovascular technologist/technician. A cardiovascular technologist performs stent implants, cardiac pacemakers, defibrillators, and other tests to diagnose heart disease. A cardiovascular technician (also known as an EKG technician) performs electrocardiograms, stress testing, and Holter monitors. Education: An associate or bachelor's degree and certification for a technologist. Technicians usually require less than one year of training plus certification. Average annual salary range: $27,000 to $140,000.

Diagnostic medical sonography. Uses sound waves to generate images to assess and diagnose medical conditions in the abdomen, breasts, heart, blood vessels, and musculoskeletal system. Education: An associate or bachelor's degree and certification. Annual salary: $53,000 to –$75,000.

Medical assistant. Supports physicians, podiatrists, chiropractors, and optometrists by providing administrative and clinical assistance. Education: One year of training or an associate degree. Average annual salary: $30,548.

Perfusionist. Operates the heart-lung machine while the surgeon operates on a patient's heart. Education: A bachelor's or master's degree, depending on the program, and credentialing. Annual salary: $65,000 to $135,000.

Phlebotomist. Collects blood for donation or for testing in a clinical laboratory. Education: 200 hours of training plus certification. Annual salary: $25,000 to $30,000.

Surgical technologist. Prepares patients for surgery, sets up the operating room, sterilizes instruments, and assists the surgeon. Education: One year of training or an associate degree; certification preferred. Average annual salary: $44,420.

Chiropractic

Chiropractor. Utilizes natural healing methods and manual manipulations of the spine, neck, and back to treat patients. Education: A doctor of chiropractic (DC) degree plus license. Average annual salary: $90,000.

Clinical Laboratory Sciences

Medical laboratory technician. Also called a clinical laboratory technician, this technician prepares and performs laboratory tests and procedures and records and analyzes data. Education: An associate degree and certification. Annual salary: $45,000 to $50,000.

Medical laboratory scientist. Conducts more advanced testing, such as molecular diagnostics, and microbiological and cross-matching blood tests. Education: A bachelor's degree plus certification. Annual salary: $55,000 to $60,000.

Dentistry

Dental assistant. Prepares patients for dental care, assists dentists, and performs office functions. Education: One-year or less of training; X-ray certification preferred. Average annual salary: $35,640.

Dental hygienist. Cleans teeth, provides oral health education, and identifies oral pathologies. Education: An associate degree and certification. Average annual salary: $55,303.

Dental laboratory technician. Designs and constructs corrective devices and dental prostheses. Education: An associate degree and certification. Average annual salary: $30,000 to 70,000.

Dentist. Evaluates, diagnoses, prevents, and treats disease disorders and conditions of the teeth and mouth. Education: A doctor of dental surgery (DDS) or doctor of dental medicine (DDM) degree plus license. Average annual salary: $214,070.

Dietetics and Nutrition

Dietetic technician. Implements nutritional and dietetic plans to patients under the supervision of a registered dietician. Education: Less than one year of training. Average annual salary for four years or less experience: $30,000 to $63,000.

Registered dietitian. Assesses, educates, manages, and prepares nutrition plans and programs. Education: A bachelor's or graduate degree plus license. Average annual salary: $63,700.

Emergency Services

Emergency medical technician (EMT). Provides immediate lifesaving care and basic, noninvasive interventions for critical patients. Advanced EMTs can also conduct limited advanced and pharmacological interventions. Education: Less than one year of training plus license. Average annual salary: $31,020.

Paramedic. The most skilled emergency responder. A paramedic is trained in performing invasive and pharmacological interventions. Education: An associate degree and license. Average annual salary: $31,020.

Health and Physical Education

Athletic trainer. Prevents, evaluates, and treats sports injuries. Education: Bachelor's degree; master's degree will be preferred in the future. Average annual salary: $55,036.

Exercise physiologist. Applies the basics of human anatomy, physiology, biochemistry, and biophysics of human movement to exercise and therapeutic rehabilitation. Education: Bachelor's degree; master's degree for some settings. Average annual salary: $30,000 and $73,000, respectively.

Kinesiotherapist. A kinesiotherapist "[d]evelops and monitors exercise programs to help people regain muscle strength and function lost due to injury or disease."[5] Education: Bachelor's degree plus certification. National average salary: $78,000.

Geriatric Care

Geriatrician. A medical doctor specifically trained to evaluate, treat, and manage the unique health-care needs of older people. Education: Medical school followed by a three-year residency usually in internal or family medicine, fellowship, license, and board certification. Annual salary: $160,000 to $200,000.

Nursing

Certified nurse assistant. Under a nurse's supervision, provides personal care to patients in nursing homes, assisted living, hospice, hospitals, community-based long-term care, correctional institutions, and other long-term care settings. Education: Graduation from a state-approved CNA program and pass a certification exam. Average annual salary: $25,620.

Certified nurse midwife. An advanced practice registered nurse who provides counseling and care during preconception, pregnancy, childbirth, and the postpartum period. Education: A registered nursing degree, completion of graduate program, plus certification. Average annual salary: $70,000.

Licensed practical nurse. Also called licensed vocational nurse (LVN) in Texas and California. Provides basic bedside care to patients under the supervision of RNs or physicians. Education: One-year diploma program and license. Average annual salary: $31,440.

Nurse anesthetist. An advanced practice nurse who provides anesthetics for surgical, obstetrical, and trauma care. Education: A bachelor's degree in nursing, minimum of one-year acute care nursing experience degree plus master's degree and national certification. Annual salary: $157,000 to $214,000.

Nurse practitioner. An advance practice registered nurse who performs many of the same functions as a physician including physical examinations, diagnosing and treating common illnesses and injuries, administering immunizations, ordering and interpreting common diagnostic tests, prescribing medications, and educating and counseling patients and their families regarding their health and health-care options. Education: A bachelor's degree in nursing degree plus graduate degree and license; doctorate degree preferred. Average annual salary: $90,583.

Registered nurse. Provides patient care under a physician's orders. Education: An associate or bachelor's degree in nursing plus state license. Average annual salary: $64,690.

Orthotics and Prosthetics

Orthotics and prosthetics. Helps patients who have lost limbs or suffered injury or impairment regain their mobility by fitting them with artificial limbs (prostheses) or orthopedic braces (orthoses). Education: Master's degree and certification. Average annual salary: $75,300.[6]

Orthotic and prosthetic assistant. Under the supervision of a certified practitioner, this technician works with patients to fabricate, repair, and maintain orthotic and prosthetic devices. Education: Less than one year of training. Average annual salary: $43,000.[7]

Pharmacy

Pharmacist. Prepares and dispenses prescription medication to patients and provides drug education or information. Education: A doctor of pharmacy degree (PharmD); national and state licenses. Average annual salary: $107,403.

Pharmacy technician. Provides customer service to pharmacy clients under the supervision of a licensed pharmacist. Education: Less than one year of training to an associate degree. Average annual salary: $25,625.

Physician

Physician. Examines, diagnoses, and treats patients in solo or group practices, hospitals, outpatient clinics, and health-care centers. Some physicians teach or do research. Education: A doctor of medicine (MD) or a doctor of osteopathic medicine (DO) degree, a three- to five-year residency program, a national license, a state license, and board certification. Average annual salary for an allopathic physician: $197,000 to $747,000; osteopathic physician: $204,000 to $443,000.

Physician assistant. Diagnoses and treats patients under the supervision of a physician. Education: A bachelor's degree plus license. Average annual salary: $94,348.

Surgeon. A physician who is specifically trained to perform surgical procedures on patients. Education: A doctorate of medicine (MD) or a doctorate of osteopathic medicine (DO), a five-year residency program, a national license, and a state license. Average compensation: $400,000 to 800,000. Plastic surgeons complete three years of general surgery residency, plus two to three years of plastic surgery residency training. Annual salary: $363,858 with a range of $307,708 to $431,843.[8]

Podiatry

Podiatrist. A physician who specializes in the prevention, diagnosis, and treatment of foot disorders. Education: A medical degree, four years of residency, a national license, a state license, and board certification. Average annual salary: $190,675.

Radiology

Health physicist. Monitors and controls radiation exposure and implements preventative measures in health care, work, and natural environments. Education: A bachelor's degree. Average annual salary: $75,467.[9]

Medical dosimetrist. Administers radiation therapy to cancer patients. Education: A bachelor's degree, preferably in the physical sciences, plus a 12- to 24-month dosimetry training program and certification. Average annual salary: $81,000 to $112,000.

Nuclear medicine technologist. A highly specialized health-care professional who prepares and administers radiopharmaceuticals to patients and monitors the affected tissues or organs. Nuclear medicine technologists may also operate computed tomography (CT) and magnetic resonance imaging (MRI) scanners. Education: An associate degree; bachelor's degree preferred. Average annual salary: $65,000.

Radiologist. A specialized physician who reads and interprets X-ray and digital images. Education: A medical degree, four years of residency, a national license, a state license, and board certification. Average annual salary: $383,249.[10]

Radiologic technologist. Operates radiologic scanning machines. These machines include X-ray machines, CT scanners (computed tomography), MRI, or mammography machines. Education: Minimum of an associate degree plus certification. Average annual salary: $62,761.

Therapy

Acupuncture. Acupuncture is a form of alternative medicine that treats patients through a variety of therapies such as needling, cupping, acupressure, exercises, and Chinese herbal preparations. Education: Three years of acupuncture training or four years for the combination of acupuncture and Eastern medicine. Must have an associate or bachelor's degree prior to training. Average annual salary: $52,000.

Audiologist. Nonmedical diagnosis and management of disorders of the auditory and balance systems. Education: A doctoral degree and certification. Median annual salary: $61,000 to $96,000.

Massage therapist. Applies manual techniques for manipulating skin, muscles, and connective tissues. Education: Less than one year of training plus certification. Average annual salary: $29,250.

Occupational therapist. Helps people of all ages to develop and recover activities of daily living such as dressing, cooking, eating, and driving. Education: A master's degree and license. Average annual salary: $82,194.[11]

Occupational therapy assistant. Works with clients under the supervision of an occupational therapist. Education: An associate degree plus certification. Average annual salary: $54,978.[12]

Physical therapist. Helps patients restore function, improve mobility, relieve pain, and prevent or limit the loss of mobility due to injury or illness. Education: A master's degree is required, doctorate preferred, and license. Average annual salary: $83,999.

Physical therapy assistant. Provides physical therapy to patients under the supervision of a licensed physical therapist. Education: An associate degree and certification. Average annual salary: $45,000.

Respiratory therapist. Helps people who suffer from chronic respiratory diseases like asthma, bronchitis, and emphysema breathe more easily. Also provides respiratory therapy to patients who have had heart attacks and have sleep disorders and to premature babies. Education: An associate degree and certification. Average annual salary: $62,223.

Speech-language pathologist. Diagnoses and treats speech, language, and swallowing disorders in children and adults. Education: A master's degree plus certification and a state license. Average annual salary: $61,000 to 71,000.

Vision Care

Ophthalmologist. Diagnoses and treats eye diseases, performs eye surgery, and prescribes and fits eyeglasses and contact lenses to correct vision problems. Education: A medical degree, residency, a national license, a state license, and board certification. Average annual salary: $273,088.[13]

Optometrist. Examines, diagnoses, treats, and manages diseases, injuries, and disorders of the eye and visual system. Optometrists differ from ophthalmologists because they are not medical doctors and cannot perform eye surgery. Education: A doctor of optometry (OD) degree plus license. Average annual salary: $122,667.

(The data for all salaries, unless otherwise noted, are from the Explore Health Careers website at http://www.explorehealthcareers.org).[14]

Human Services Careers

People in human services occupations are interested in working with people to resolve personal and societal issues. People in these occupations value helping others and have high interpersonal skills. They are

Table 5.2   Job Titles at the Bachelor's Degree Level

• Case worker	• Family support worker
• Youth worker	• Social service liaison
• Residential counselor	• Social service technician
• Adult day care worker	• Alcohol or drug abuse counselor
• Life skills instructor	• Client advocate
• Probation officer	• Therapeutic assistant
• Child advocate	• Rehabilitation case worker
• Group home worker	• Juvenile court liaison
• Child abuse worker	• Crisis intervention counselor
• Mental health aide	• Community organizer
• Intake interviewer	• Community outreach worker
• Social work assistant	• Community action worker
• Psychological aide	• Halfway house counselor
• Residential manager	

friendly, trusting, and warm; enjoy working with others; and prefer team approaches.

An associate degree in human services can be a starting point to a career in human services and will qualify you for the following entry-level positions:

- Social service/social work/case management aide/assistant
- Residential program technician or residential aide worker
- Community support or outreach worker
- Mental health technician

A master's degree is required to provide counseling or therapy. The median annual human services worker salary is $26,582, with a range of $22,433 to $32,089.[15] For more detailed job descriptions and current salary figures, visit Salary.com.

Social Work Careers

The field of social work uses social theories to understand and improve individual's lives and society as a whole. Social workers can specialize in a particular area such as child welfare, aging, addiction, health, or social justice. They work with children, individuals, families, couples, the elderly, communities, and organizations. Social workers protect and act as advocates for their clients, connect clients to resources in the community, educate and teach life skills, and counsel clients.

Job Titles:

- Child, family, and school social workers
- Medical and public health social workers
- Mental health social workers
- Substance abuse social workers

The master of social work (MSW) degree is the minimum degree requirement to become a licensed social worker. There are entry-level positions in social work for individuals who have bachelor's degrees in psychology, sociology, or education. These individuals are generally supervised by a licensed social worker. However, only individuals with an MSW degree are able to provide counseling services.

How much does a social worker (BSW) make? According to Salary .com, the median annual social worker's (BSW) salary is $53,350, with a range of $47,194 to $59,793.[16]

Counseling Careers

According to the American Counseling Association, "Professional Counselors are graduate level (either master's or doctoral degree) mental health service providers who are trained to work with individuals, families, and groups in treating mental, behavioral, and emotional problems and disorders."[17]

Table 5.3   Job Titles

• Community/mental health counselor	• Marriage, couple, and family counselor
• Employment/vocational/career counselor	• Rehabilitation counselor
• Addictions and behavioral counselor	• School counselor
• Life counselor/coach	• Grief counselor
• Pastoral/spiritual counselor	• Domestic violence counselor
• Gerontological counselor	• Student affairs and college counselor

Counselors can specialize in a variety of areas. Some counselors, like myself (a college career counselor), work in colleges and universities as academic advisors, residence life coordinators, or personal counselors.

A licensed professional counselor can also work in private practice. The average pay for a mental health counselor is $39,119 per year.[18] Counselors who work in higher education can make considerably more.

Psychology Careers

One of the latest areas of interest in the field of psychology is neuropsychology. New research in neuroscience and cognitive science is showing evidence that counseling can build new brain networks. In the future, counselors and psychologists will be able to harness neuroscience to treat their clients during therapy.

A PhD or PsyD degree is required to practice as a licensed psychologist. Doctoral-level psychologists can also conduct psychological research and teach at colleges and universities. Individuals with a master's degree in psychology can work as industrial-organizational psychologists or as research assistants under the direct supervision of a doctoral-level psychologist. Individuals with a bachelor's degree in psychology can assist psychologists and other mental health professionals in community mental health centers, vocational rehabilitation offices, and correctional programs. Others can find entry-level employment in sales, customer service, or business management.

How much does a licensed psychologist make? The median annual salary is $88,951, with a range of $79,219 to $101,204.[19]

Table 5.4   Specialty Areas in Psychology

• School psychology	• Clinical psychology
• Neuropsychology	• Developmental psychology
• Child psychology	• Forensic psychology
• Industrial/organizational psychology	• Cognitive psychology
• Social psychology	• Rehabilitation psychology
• Geropsychology	• Health psychology
• Counseling psychology	• Experimental/research psychology
• Sports psychology	

Funeral Director

Being a funeral director is an honorable and compassionate career choice. Funeral directors, also called morticians, supervise or conduct the preparation of the dead for burial or cremation and direct or arrange funerals. Funeral directors have the delicate task of handling the family members of the deceased individual in a compassionate, delicate, and calming manner. In addition, they must have excellent organization skills and keep up to date with the latest industry-related details. Funeral directors must be able to handle the emotional aspects of their profession and possess a natural empathy and desire to help those who are grieving through a difficult and painful process.

To become a mortician, you must graduate from a two-year or four-year mortuary program and pass a licensing exam. The average salary for a funeral director is $44,064 per year.[20]

CHAPTER SIX

Careers for Analytical People

Deprived of meaningful work, men and women lose their reason for existence.

—Fyodor Dostoevsky

How Do I Know If I'm an Analytical Thinker?

If you are an analytical thinker, you will probably like working with ideas and theories. You prefer to approach things in a logical and systematic manner and you enjoy solving problems. Analytical thinkers are usually intellectual, inquisitive people who enjoy searching for facts and understanding of the world around them.

Analytical thinkers are usually drawn to fields such as IT, engineering, science, and research.

Green Careers

Green careers and jobs are commonly associated with alternative energy, building, and manufacturing but can include any occupation that is affected by conserving energy, developing alternative energy, reducing pollution, or recycling. The renewed interest in finding and developing new sources of energy (biofuels, electric cars, solar, wind generation, clean coal, etc.) and the attention on environmental sustainability has produced a whole new generation of jobs that until a few years ago didn't previously exist. Jobs like green interior designers, environmental lawyers, wind turbine technicians, solar panel installers, and energy auditors have emerged in response to green trends. Other positions have sprung up within existing or traditional engineering and science careers (green architects, green landscape architects, green construction, water-resource engineers, sustainable food production, etc.). Green marketing, or eco-marketing, is a relatively new field that refers to the process of selling products and services based on their environmental benefits. Examples of green marketing are promoting products that are made from renewable materials or restaurants that advertise serving only "locally sourced" food. My family recently switched to growth hormone free milk based on those reasons.

Green jobs can be found in the state and federal government; private industry; new start-up alternative energy companies; and engineering firms, construction companies, and manufacturing plants. Environmental consulting and environmental activist groups are also big employers for green jobs.[1] The Bureau of Labor Statistics has a series of green career articles that can be accessed at http://www.bls.gov/green /greencareers.htm.

The green movement has touched almost every aspect of our business world as companies try to produce goods and services with less environmental impact. No doubt there will be more green jobs and careers created after this book is published, so stay tuned!

Stem Careers

Science, technology, engineering, and mathematics (STEM) is an acronym that refers to the academic disciplines of science, technology, engineering, and mathematics. Recently, there has been a lot of talk about STEM careers and the need for employees, especially women, in those fields. Data from the White House found that "women and minorities account for 70 percent of all college students, but only 45 percent of students in STEM majors."[2]

According to the National Association of Colleges and Employers (NACE) 2016 winter survey, "[M]ore than half of the employers responding to the *Job Outlook 2016* survey noted plans to hire 2016 graduates with bachelor's degrees in the STEM fields, making these grads among the mostly highly sought in the class."[3]

"Engineering graduates from the class of 2017 are expected to be the highest paid with an overall average salary projection of $66,097."[4] The report also states that computer science graduates' salary projections are up from last year by almost 7 percent. Math and science degrees are also in high demand and salaries are expected to average just over $60,000.

Life sciences have proved to be a relatively buoyant market in 2016, as government health-care policies, drug regulations, and merger and acquisition activities contribute to hiring movements in the sector.[5] Upper-level positions usually require a PhD. If you prefer a nonlaboratory environment, product/sales specialists are expected to be in demand as well.

Careers in Computers

Within the field of information technology, computer support specialists assist developers, analysts, administrators, and end users. Help desk technicians assist the public with questions and problems regarding their computers. An associate degree is usually the entry-level educational requirement.

Computer programmers, computer analysts, and software developers typically have a bachelor's in computer science, but IT and database managers and network systems administrators can have a bachelor's degree in computer science or information science.

According to the latest Bureau of Labor Statistics projections for 2014–2024, the employment of computer systems analysts and software, applications, and systems developers are expected to grow faster than the average for all occupations.[6] This growth is primarily due to our increased reliance on computers and the growing demand in software for cloud computing, cybersecurity, and mobile networks.

The use of mobile apps is so hot right now that every entertainment, lifestyle, education, and telecom industry is scrambling to develop mobile and game apps. As a result, there are a number of career opportunities opening up in the mobile and technology industry.[7]

Table 6.1   Jobs in the Computer Industry

Software Development	
Artificial intelligence programmer	Bioinformatics specialist
Database analyst	Data miner
Programmer	Project manager
Software engineer	Systems analyst
Systems consultant	Systems programmer
IT Operation and Management	
Computer operator	Chief information officer
Cybersecurity specialist	Database administrator
Manager	Systems administrator

(Continued)

Table 6.1   (Continued)

Training and Support

Help desk support technician	Manager, technical support
Recruiter	Service technician
Technical editor/writer	Trainer, software applications

Manufacturing

Computer-aided design technician	Computer hardware designer/engineer
Computer systems designer	Robotics engineer

Academic IT Professions

Curriculum or media specialist	Computer services manager
Network specialist	Professor, computer science/ITs
Reference librarian	Webpage designer/manager

Web and Internet

Application developer	Database developer
Internet consultant	Webmaster
Webpage designer	

Graphics and Multimedia

Art director (computer graphics)	Animation programmer
Computer graphics artist/designer	Computer graphics technician
Game designer/programmer	Multimedia developer
Multimedia or game writer/editor	Playtester, computer games
Virtual reality designer/programmer	

Networking

Network administrator	Network analyst
Network control operator	Telecommunications engineer

Computer Industry Specialists

Computer store owner or manager	Industry analyst, computer products
Sales manager, computer products	Sales representative, computer products

Mobile

Android software developer	iOS developer
Mobile app developer	Mobile sales executive

For graduates armed with a degree in computer science or IT, there's one thing that's clear—you are in demand. Average salaries in computer science start around $66,000; information sciences just over $64,500, and software applications at $66,000.[8] Mobile applications developers in the United States can expect to earn an average salary of $72,000 annually.[9] (See Payscale.com for the latest salary figures.)

Careers in Conservation and the Environment

Do you care about global warming? Do you have a passion for teaching others how to preserve and appreciate our natural world? If so, then you may be interested in a career in environmental policy, education, conservation, renewable energy, or engineering. According to Environmental Science.org, "Environmental scientists conduct research to identify, control, or eliminate sources of pollutants or hazards affecting the environment or public health."[10] Some scientists also develop plans to fix environmental hazards or serve as advisors to the governmental officials who make policies.

Table 6.2 Jobs in Conservation and the Environment

Ecotourism	
Camp director	Outfitter
Resort manager	River guide
Tour guide	Wilderness guide

Engineering	
Biological and agricultural engineer	Community planner
Environmental engineer	Geospatial engineer
Mining and geological engineer	Surveyor

Farming and Fishing	
Agricultural consultant	Commercial beekeeper
Crop farmer	Crop scientist
Dairy farmer	Farm manager
Fish farmer	Livestock farmer

Forestry	
Forester	Forestry technician
Logger	Urban forester

(Continued)

Table 6.2   (Continued)

Legal and Regulatory

Environmental attorney	Environmental campaign staff worker
Environmental compliance specialist	Environmental economist
Environmental health officer	Fish and wildlife officer
Irrigation auditor	Occupational safety and health officer
Park manager	

Other

Landscape architect	Nature photographer/writer

Outdoor/Environmental Education

Ecological restoration instructor	Environmental education director
Environmental science teacher/professor	Field education coordinator
Field teacher/naturalist	Forestry professor
Marine science instructor	Outdoor education instructor
Recreation and fitness studies professor	Recreation planner

Scientific

Atmospheric scientist	Chemical laboratory technician
Environmental chemist	Environmental technician
Geoscientist	Marine biologist
Marine science technician	Oceanographer
Plant scientist	Range manager
Soil scientist	Veterinarian
Wetland scientist	Wildlife rehabilitator
Wildlife scientist	

Careers in Engineering

Are you wondering if engineering may be right for you? The Tryengineering.org website has some handy questions to ask yourself:

- Do you like to solve problems?
- Do you like math and science?
- Do you like to think of new ways to do things?
- Do you like puzzles and other mind challenging games?

- Do you like working with computers?
- Do you enjoy a challenge?
- Do you want to make a difference in the world?
- Do you have an interest in the challenges facing our world?
- Do you want to help people and improve their lives?
- Do you wonder how things work?[11]

If you found yourself agreeing to several of these questions, then engineering might be the profession for you.

Engineers apply scientific and mathematical principles to solve problems and creating things that improve our lives. They design bridges and medical equipment as well as processes for cleaning up environmental waste and build systems for mass transit.

There is a difference between traditional engineering programs that always lead to a bachelor's degree or higher and engineering technology that can be earned at the associate degree or the bachelor's degree level. Traditional engineering is more theoretical in nature, requires a higher level of math and physics courses, and focuses on design or research. Engineering technology is more practical and bridges the gap between technicians and engineers. Engineering technologists focus on the installation, maintenance, testing, and operation of components and instruments.

There are many different types of engineering jobs to choose from: development, design, testing, research, and sales positions. If you are interested in discovering something new, you might consider a career as a research engineer. If you are imaginative and creative, you may be more interested in design engineering. If you like laboratory courses and conducting experiments, you may want to become a development engineer. Engineering sales or management might be a good choice if you have good communication skills and enjoy working with people.

There are five main branches of engineering: chemical, civil, electrical, industrial, and mechanical engineering. But that's not all—there are also a number of specialized engineering fields: aerospace, agricultural, architectural, biomedical, ceramics, computer, electromechanical, environmental, geological, marine, materials, metallurgical, mining, nanotechnology, nuclear, photonics, and surveying engineering.

Aerospace engineering. Aerospace engineering is one of the newest branches of engineering and deals with the development of aircraft and spacecraft. Aerospace vehicle systems are used for exploration, infrastructure, and defense applications. Aerospace engineers design, analyze, and test airplanes, helicopters, satellites, missiles, and jet- and rocket-propulsion systems. Average starting salary: $64,967.

Agricultural and biological engineering. Agricultural engineers, also called biological and agricultural engineers, analyze agricultural operations; design environmentally sound land and water conservation systems; develop new food processing methods; and create safer, more effective agricultural equipment and structures. Agricultural engineers work in the farming, forestry, and food processing industries. They also investigate ways of improving agricultural production and processing in developing countries. Average starting salary: $57,841.[12]

Architectural engineering. Architectural engineers apply scientific and engineering principles to the design and construction of buildings and structures. Architectural engineering focuses on structural aspects of building, while architecture focuses on the aesthetics and functional layout of buildings. Average starting salary: $57,164.[13]

Biomedical engineering. Bioengineers, or biomedical engineers, apply engineering techniques and methods to advance health care and solve problems in medicine and biology. The pacemaker was developed by bioengineers. Average starting salary: $67,250.

Chemical engineering. "Chemical Engineers apply the principles of chemistry, biology, physics, and math to solve problems that involve the production or use of chemicals, fuel, drugs, food, and many other products."[14] Chemical engineers develop new ways to manufacture a variety of products from medicines and plastics to household soap. They also design large-scale chemical manufacturing plants or specialize in a particular chemical process such as oxidation or a particular field such as nanomaterials or biotechnology. Average starting salary: $68,445.

Civil engineering. Civil engineers plan, design, construct, operate, and maintain roads and highways, buildings, airports, bridges, tunnels, dams and levees, and wastewater collection and treatment systems. When designing and constructing structures and buildings, civil engineers work closely with other professionals such as architects and contractors. Average starting salary: $63,563.

Computer engineering. Computer engineers research, design, develop, test, and oversee the manufacture and installation of all of the components that make up computers, such as computer chips, circuit boards, keyboards, routers, and printers. The field of computer engineering is similar to electronics engineering in that they both design and test circuits, but computer engineers are concerned only with computers and computer-related equipment.[15] Average starting salary: $68,191.

Electrical engineering. One of the broadest engineering majors, electrical engineering integrates electricity and electronic devices into all facets of our daily lives. Electrical and electronics engineers work on a wide range of technologies: portable music players, household appliances, 'smart" lighting in buildings, the electrical systems inside automobiles and aircrafts, telecommunication systems, electric power stations, and satellite communications.

Electrical engineers typically focus on products that supply, generate, or transmit electricity. In contrast, electronics engineers focus on electronic components or equipment. Average starting salary: $66,920.

Environmental engineering. Environmental engineers use the principles of biology and chemistry to develop solutions to environmental problems such as water and air pollution, recycling, waste management and disposal, and other public health issues. Average starting salary: $63,190.

Industrial engineering. Industrial engineers determine the most productive ways to make products or provide services by efficiently using people, machines, materials, information, and energy. Industrial engineers work to develop the best way to manufacture a particular product; enable managers to make more effective decisions in scheduling, inventory, and quality control; and design processes that enable work to be performed more safely, comfortably, and efficiently. Average starting salary: $64,280.

Materials engineering. Materials engineers are responsible for producing the materials that make up all of our modern devices: machines, computers, automobiles, aircraft, communication equipment, and other products. Materials engineers not only develop new materials but improve and produce traditional materials reliably and economically. Average starting salary: $66,970.

Mechanical engineering. Mechanical engineering is one of the oldest branches of engineering. Mechanical engineering deals with all aspects of mechanics, energy, and heat. They research, create, manufacture, and test tools, engines, machines, home appliances, rocket engines, air conditioning equipment, nuclear and steam power plants, just to name a few. Average starting salary: $65,557.

Nuclear engineering. Nuclear engineers focus on the benefits of nuclear energy and radiation. They design and build nuclear power plants, develop nuclear power sources for naval vessels or spacecraft, design medical imaging devices and medical diagnostics equipment, set standards and develop radiation detection and measurement methods, and develop ways to monitor and dispose of radioactive waste. Starting salary $63,730.

Petroleum engineering. Petroleum engineers search the world for reservoirs containing oil or natural gas and design ways to extract those natural resources. Average starting salary: $77,000.

Surveying engineering. Surveying is one of the oldest professions in the world. It has traditionally been defined as the science, art, and technology of accurately determining relative positions of points and extent of features and phenomena above, on, or below the surface of the Earth and for establishing such point and features on the ground. Surveying may be regarded as that discipline which encompasses all methods for measuring or acquiring data about physical features of the Earth, processing them and communicating the derived information in a variety of formats. Subdisciplines in land surveying include boundary surveying, construction surveying, geodetic surveying, photogrammetry, remote sensing, and hydrographic surveying. Boundary surveyors provide expert opinions on ownership and extent of existing properties. They are the only professionals authorized by virtue of their license, to create and retrace existing boundaries, to subdivide single parcels into two or more parcels of properties, and to retrace the extent of existing property boundaries. Construction surveyors accurately translate the designs of architects and engineers from paper to the ground and control the alignment and grade for such projects. They manage and direct small and large construction projects ranging from a simple building foot print layout to high-rises, roads, pipelines, bridges, dams, and other construction projects. Geodesists monitor the physical characteristics of the Earth and its interrelationship with other planets. Such characteristics include the Earth's geometry, gravity field, its orbital motion, and plate dynamics. Photogrammetrists make precise measurements from imagery, whether analog or digital, that have been acquired from air- and space-borne platforms such as unmanned aerial vehicles (UAVs), planes, and satellites. They produce topographic maps, orthophotomaps, digital terrain models, and other products, which are used by the general public and other professionals. Remote sensing is a discipline similar to photogrammetry except the images are obtained using various regions of the electromagnetic spectrum including visible light. They create thematic maps that help scientists to understand natural phenomena and the impacts of human activities or natural disasters on the environment. Hydrographic surveyors measure the depths of water bodies such as lakes and oceans to create accurate maps of the bottoms of these features, which are used for safe navigation and by sportsmen.

A professional land surveyor's average salary is $66,061, with a range of $49,508 to $93,200.[16]

Note: Average starting salaries are from the National Association of Colleges and Employers (NACE) Winter 2017 Salary Survey.[17]

The minimum educational requirement for entry-level positions in all types of engineering is a bachelor's degree, but higher-level management or research positions may require a graduate degree. Engineering technologists generally have an associate or a bachelor's degree in engineering technology and are more application oriented than traditional engineers.

For more details about careers in engineering, visit the Career Cornerstone website at http://www.careercornerstone.org.

Careers in Forensics

Although often associated with solving murders in popular television shows like NCIS, the term "forensics" can be applied to any field that uses scientific tests or techniques to detect crime. The FBI uses forensic accountants and auditors to review tax records to determine if embezzlement or any other white-collar crime has occurred. Digital forensics is the process of uncovering and interpreting electronic data—what an IT professional does to recover computer files that may have been deleted or damaged.

Contrary to popular belief, popular TV shows such as *CSI*, *NCIS*, *Law and Order*, and *Bones* misrepresent the forensics profession in many ways. Forensic scientists don't spend all of their time solving murders, and only do the police interrogate suspects and make arrests. Typically, toxicology tests can take four to six weeks to complete.[18] The other big surprise for students is that a forensic science degree requires a substantial amount of science and math courses in college.

Forensic scientists can find employment in government or law enforcement agencies, as independent consultants, or at private forensic laboratories. Salary ranges tend to vary among these industries; however, federal agencies, such as the FBI, generally offer higher salaries. A forensic accountant earns an average salary around $65,000 per year,[19] and a forensic pathologist, according to 2016 PayScale.com figures, earns around $100,000.[20]

Visit the American Forensics Association (http://www.americanforensics.org) for more information about career opportunities in the field of forensics.

Table 6.3   Jobs in Forensic Science

Crime Scene and Criminal Investigation

Crime scene investigator	Crime scene supervisor
Criminal investigator	Evidence custodian
Fingerprint technician	Fire investigator
Patrol officer	Polygraph examiner

Crime Lab

Crime lab director	Crime lab supervisor
Crime lab technician	Criminalist

Criminalists

Bloodstain pattern analyst	DNA analyst
Firearms examiner	Forensic biologist
Forensic chemist	Forensic drug chemist
Forensic serologist	Latent print examiner
Questioned document examiner	Trace evidence examiner

Medical, Legal, and Death Investigation

Accident reconstruction specialist	Construction forensics expert
Coroner	Forensic anthropologist
Forensic architect	Forensic pathologist
Forensic surveyor	Forensic toxicologist
Medical examiner	

Educators, Researchers, and Reporters

Crime reporter	Forensic science instructor
Forensic science researcher	Forensic training specialist

Careers in Mathematics

There are many career opportunities in mathematics. Examples include occupations that apply math in business, biology, computer science, education, engineering, research, and development. People in these occupations are creative thinkers who apply mathematical principles to solve problems and research new ideas. If you enjoy mathematics courses, consider the following career options. Websites for additional research in each career are also included in each section.

Actuarial Science

Actuaries manage risk. They apply the principles of statistics to finance, insurance, and other industries that seek to analyze risk. This job is consistently rated as one of the top two careers in terms of job satisfaction, opportunities for advancement, and pay. Actuaries are well compensated—they can expect to earn an average of $82,000 annually, with a range of $50,000–$135,000.[21] Depending on the college or university, students can find the actuarial science major in the mathematics or business departments.

For more information about the field of actuarial science, visit the Actuarial Professional Society (http://www.beanactuary.org).

Operations Research

Operations research (OR) is a scientific approach to analyzing business problems like costs or profits and making decisions. Much of this work is done using statistical analysis and mathematical modeling techniques to analyze complex situation. To qualify for positions in OR, you will need a bachelor's degree in mathematics, followed by a master's degree. Operations researchers can find employment in government and policy agencies or the pharmaceutical, airline, IT, logistics, and financial services industries. According to the Bureau of Labor Statistics, "Employment of operations research analysts is projected to grow 30 percent from 2014 to 2024, much faster than the average for all occupations."[22]

The Operations Research Professional Society (http://www.informs.org) contains more information about a career in this field.

Applied Mathematics

Accounting, economics, engineering, computer science, finance, medicine, physics, and astronomy all use mathematics. If you enjoy mathematics but are looking for a career outside of education or research, then you may be interested in one of the "applied" mathematical fields. To learn more about careers in applied mathematics, visit the Society for Industrial and Applied Mathematics (SIAM) (http://www.siam.org), the Mathematical Association of America (http://www.maa.org), or the American Mathematics Society (http://www.ams.org).

Statistics

According to the World of Statistics, "Statisticians provide crucial guidance in determining what information is reliable and which predictions can be trusted."[23] They work in a variety of fields including medicine, government, education, agriculture, business, and law. There is a high demand for statisticians, but most jobs require an advanced degree in statistics. Average annual salary: $50,000.[24]

For more information about the field of statistics, visit the Statistical Professional Society (http://www.amstat.org).

Mathematical Biology

Today's fastest-growing fields are where mathematics, computer science, biology, and medicine intersect. Mathematical biology, also known as bioinformatics, uses mathematics to build models of biological processes that can be used in cellular neurobiology, epidemic modeling, and population genetics. Most jobs require an advanced degree.

For more information about the field of bioinformatics, visit the Society for Mathematical Biology (http://www.smb.org).

The U.S. government, especially the CIA and NSA, is the country's leading employer of mathematicians with positions at all educational levels. Many of these mathematicians are employed to design and analyze complex algorithms and to develop and analyze cryptographs. There are also jobs for math majors in other government agencies including defense, social security, internal revenue, and the census bureau.

Middle school and high school mathematics teachers will continue to be in high demand. Earning a master's degree in mathematics or mathematics education will enable you to teach at many community colleges, while a PhD will prepare you to teach and do research at the university level.

Research mathematicians can find teaching and research positions at colleges and universities or at large companies such as Microsoft, Boeing, and Google.

For more information about teaching careers in math, visit the National Council of Teachers of Mathematics (K–12) (http://www.nctm.org) or the American Mathematical Association of Two Year Colleges (http://www.amatyc.org).

Mathematicians take home approximately $78,000 per year on average. Overall incomes of mathematicians are spread between $45,000 and $134,000 depending on individual performance.[25]

Careers in Science

Science occupations deal with research and the application of scientific knowledge to solving problems, inventing new technologies, and developing new products. People in these occupations usually have good problem-solving skills and value inventiveness, accuracy, achievement, and independence. They may be described as curious, logical, precise, analytical, and reserved.

Science is a broad field and is made up of a wide range of subspecialties from botany to zoology. The following are brief definitions of the more popular science occupations including the amount of training required and average annual salary. The salaries listed are from the National Association of Colleges and Employers Winter 2016 Salary Survey.[26] Note that salaries for graduates with bachelor's degrees are generally low because a master's or PhD is the preferred degree in these fields. For current job outlook information, check the *Occupational Outlook Handbook* at www.ooh.gov, published every two years by the U.S. Bureau of Labor Statistics.

Agricultural Science

Agricultural science is a broad multidisciplinary field. Agriculture is the science and practice of farming animals and plants for human use and consumption. Agricultural scientists study and research ways to improve the efficiency and safety of agriculture.

Some colleges offer associate degrees in turf grass management, forest technology, agricultural business, wildlife technology, food science and other areas for those who want to become technicians. Bachelor's degree programs are required for those who wish to work in the industry or on farms or ranches or pursue graduate work. Teaching and research positions require a master's degree or a PhD. Average starting salary: $51,500.

The following are some of the subdisciplines within the agricultural sciences: agronomy (the study of crop production and soil management), agricultural biotechnology (the use of scientific techniques, including genetic engineering, to modify plants, animals, and microorganisms), animal science (the study of domestic livestock—beef cattle, dairy cattle, poultry, sheep, swine, horses, goats, buffalo, emus, ostriches, llamas—wildlife, fish, laboratory animals, pets, and zoo animals), food science (the study and research of the composition and properties of foods, ingredients, and additives), forestry and wildlife ecology (the study and management of forests, wood and wood products, wildlife, and fish), horticulture (the science of growing edible and ornamental plants for gardens and landscaping, including fruits, vegetables, herbs, spices, flowers, shrubs, trees, ground covers, and turf grass), and soil science (the study of soils and soil environments).

Biology

Biology is the study of how all living organisms function. There are several subdisciplines of biology. These include biochemistry (the study of how chemicals combine and react within cells), bioinformatics (the scientific management of biological information stored in computer databases), botany (the study of the plant world), cellular biology (the study of cells), ecology (the study of how ecosystems are organized and interact with one another), entomology (the study of insects), genetics (the study of how traits are passed on through generations), marine biology (the study of marine animals), microbiology (the study of bacteria, viruses, fungi, and other microorganisms), molecular biology (the study of how genetic information is read and controlled), physiology (the study of how living organisms function), and zoology (the study of the animal kingdom).[27] There are several career paths that biologists can follow: research, health care, environmental management, biotechnology, and education. A bachelor's degree and often an advanced degree, such as a master's degree, are needed. Research jobs typically require a doctorate. Average starting salary: $51,213.

Chemistry

All matter is composed of chemical compounds. Chemistry is a physical science that studies how these chemical substances make up matter. Chemistry is divided into several major fields of study: organic chemistry (the study of carbon compounds), inorganic chemistry (the study of non-organic substances that make up matter such as minerals and metals), physical chemistry (the application of physical laws and mathematical formulas to study the physical and chemical characteristics of matter), analytical chemistry (the science of obtaining, processing, and communicating information about the composition and structure of matter), and biochemistry (the study of the chemistry of living organisms).[28] A bachelor's degree is required for research assistant and technician positions; an advanced degree is required for research and teaching positions. Average starting salary: $55,900.

Earth Science

"Earth science" is a broad term that covers four main areas: geology, meteorology, oceanography, and astronomy. We live in a time when the earth's climate is changing. Earth scientists recognize that this change is because of human activity and will play a key role in resolving this problem. There are several subdisciplines in the field of earth science:

Geology. Geology is an earth science that deals with the structure, composition, process, and history of the Earth. Geologists study the materials (rocks, minerals, and soil) that make up the Earth, the landforms (mountains, volcanoes, valleys, plains, rivers) on the Earth's surface, the rock layers and fossil remains, and the processes that shape the Earth (weather, erosion, earthquakes, tectonics). Subfields of geology include volcanology (the study of volcanoes), seismology (the study of earthquakes), hydrology (freshwater resources), and paleontology (the history of the Earth).[29] The minimum educational requirement is a bachelor's degree, but a master's degree or a PhD is preferred for teaching and research positions. Average starting salary: $43,200.

Meteorology. Meteorology is the study of the Earth's weather and climate. Broadcast meteorologists forecast the weather. Forensic meteorologists work for lawyers or insurance agencies and determine how weather conditions may have contributed to accidents or caused damage to property. Climatologist study large-scale weather patterns. The minimum educational requirement is a bachelor's degree, but a master's degree or a PhD is preferred for teaching and research positions. Average starting salary is around $43,000.

Oceanography. Oceanography is the study of the Earth's oceans. According to the national Ocean Service, "Oceanography covers a wide range of topics, including marine life and ecosystems, ocean circulation, plate tectonics and the geology of the sea floor, and the chemical and physical properties of the ocean."[30] Oceanographers usually specialize in one of four subdisciplines: Biological oceanography (the study of marine plants and animals); chemical oceanography (the study of the composition, processes, and interaction of seawater); geological oceanography (the study of the physical and chemical properties of rock and sediments found at the coastlines and on the ocean floors); and physical oceanography (the study of the motions and physical conditions in the ocean such as waves, currents, sand deposits, coastal erosion, and the ocean's interactions with its boundaries).[31] The minimum educational requirement is a bachelor's degree, but a master's degree or a PhD is preferred for teaching and research positions. Average starting salary is around $43,000.

Astronomy. In its simplest terms, astronomy is the study of the stars, planets, space, and other cosmic bodies and phenomena. Modern astronomers tend to fall into two categories: observational (observe starts, planets, galaxies, etc.) and theoretical (model and analyze how systems may have evolved). The minimum educational requirement is a bachelor's degree, but a master's degree or a PhD is preferred for teaching and research positions. Average starting salary is around $43,000.

Geography

Geography is the study of the physical processes and human activities that occur on the Earth's surface. Geographers not only study the physical features of the Earth but how people interact with and affect their environments. Geography is divided into several branches: Physical geography (physical characteristics of the Earth), human geography (people and their interaction with the Earth), regional geography (focuses on a regional area of the Earth such as an island, valley, state, or continent), cartography (map making), and geographic information systems (GISs) (geographic data stored in a computer system).[32] A bachelor's degree is required; master's degree or PhD is preferred for research and teaching positions. Average starting salary for a GIS specialist: $49,000.[33]

Physics

In its simplest terms, physics is the study of matter and energy. Physics is a fundamental science that has helped solve problems in medicine, engineering, chemistry, technology, communications, biotechnology, energy, and environmental science. There are many branches of physics: acoustics (the study of sound and sound waves), astronomy (the study of the planets, moons, stars, solar systems and galaxies, and spatial anomalies), astrophysics (the study of the physical properties of objects in space), atomic physics (the study of atoms, specifically the electron properties of the atom), biophysics (the study of physics in living systems), chemical physics (the study of physics in chemical systems), geophysics (the study of the physical properties of the Earth), nuclear physics (the study of the atomic nucleus), particle physics (the study of fundamental particles and the forces of their interaction), plasma physics (the study of highly ionized gases), space physics (the study of the physical processes of the interplanetary space environment), and quantum physics (the study of science where the smallest discrete values, or quanta, of matter and energy become relevant).[34] Most physicists are involved in theoretical or applied research in academia, government, industry, and private research laboratories. A bachelor's degree is the minimum requirement for research assistance positions, but a master's or doctoral degree is required for teaching and research positions. Average starting salary: $65,250.

Table 6.4   Jobs in Science

Biological Sciences

Bioinformatics scientist	Biologist
Botanist	Ecologist
Entomologist	Forensic scientist
Geneticist	Microbiologist
Marine biologist	Molecular biologist
Physiologist	Zoologist

Chemistry

Biochemist	Chemist
Chemical engineer	Toxicologist

Physics And Astronomy

Astronomer	Biophysicist
Nuclear physicist	Physicist
Space physicist	

Earth Sciences

Geographer	Geologist
Geophysicist	Hydrologist
Meteorologist	Meteorologist
Oceanographer	Paleontologist
Seismologist	Volcanologist

Industry

Industrial research scientist	Patent agent
Project manager	Quality control
Regulatory affairs specialist	Science technician
Technical/scientific writer	

Business

Actuary	Entrepreneur (science and technology)
Management consultant	Market research analyst
Operations research analyst	Scientific or technical sales rep

Education and Communications

College professor	Science curator
Science educator (nonschool settings)	Science and technology policy analyst
Science writer	

(*Continued*)

Table 6.4   (Continued)

Agricultural and Food Science	
Agricultural engineer	Animal scientist
Crop scientist	Food scientist
Horticultural scientist	Soil scientist

Medical Science	
Biomedical engineer	Epidemiologist
Medical physicist	Medical scientist
Pathologist	Pharmacologist

Environmental Protection and Conservation	
Environmental chemist	Environmental engineer
Environmental planner	Environmental scientist
Forester	Wildlife biologist

Career opportunities in the sciences can be found in academic and government settings, as well as in medicine, biotechnology, agriculture, food processing, energy, aviation, chemical manufacturing, fossil fuels, and the telecommunications industries. In addition to research or teaching positions, scientists can find employment as science writers, science curators, and technical advisors.

There are a wide range of jobs in the sciences, and, as expected, their pay varies greatly. A bachelor's degree is required for entry-level research and technician positions in the sciences, but an advanced degree is needed for management positions, teaching positions at colleges and universities, and research positions. See www1.salary.com/Science-and-Research-Salaries.html for the latest salary figures.

CHAPTER SEVEN

Careers for Creative People

Life isn't about finding yourself. Life is about creating yourself.
—George Bernard Shaw

How Do I Know If I'm a Creator?

If you are a creator, you will probably like working in an unstructured environment where you can create something original and unique. You may enjoy painting, drawing, creative writing, or playing an instrument. Even if you do not consider yourself an artist, you will likely enjoy experiencing art, music, and drama.

Creators are complex, paradoxical, and tend to avoid habit or routine. They prefer an environment with a good deal of freedom and flexibility to express themselves. Creators have an urge to design and create. For some people, creativity is an essential part of who they are. For creative people, the nine-to-five routine is just not a good brain fit.[1] Creative people may not be ready to produce until midday or may get another burst of energy late in the day. Frank Lloyd Wright would often wake up at 3 or 4 a.m., work several hours, and then go back to bed.[2]

In her article, *18 Things Highly Creative People Do Differently*, Carolyn Gregoire writes, "Psychologists have shown that creative people are energized by challenging activities, a sign of intrinsic motivation, and the research suggests that simply thinking of intrinsic reasons to perform an activity may be enough to boost creativity."[3] She further goes on to say that creative individuals often get into a "flow" state, a heightened state of effortless concentration and calmness that can help them create at their highest level. Creative people tend to focus on the "big" picture and can often see possibilities and connections that others don't.[4]

Creators usually choose careers in the arts, design, music, theater, writing, and performance.

Careers for Artists

Regardless of what creative career you eventually choose, you can improve your chances of success in your career by becoming the best prepared, most qualified candidate for the job. Consider earning a bachelor of fine arts (BFA) degree rather than the broader bachelor of arts degree. The BFA is considered to be the most prestigious bachelor's degree that you can receive. Research what others in your area of interest have done to prepare themselves and how they found job openings. If you're interested in flexible hours, then freelancing may be for you. Several art careers lend themselves to freelancing including fine artists, illustrators, independent curators, graphic designers, art consultants, art journalism, and art conservators and preparators. Many journalists, book authors, greeting card authors, ghost writers, and editors work on a freelance or contract basis.

If you're interested in pursuing a career in art, music, or writing, you may want to take some business and marketing courses while you're still in college. Those who have some basic business skills will have an advantage over those who don't have such skills.

Creative careers are not all about being struck by inspiration—they have their share of routine tasks as well. If you're a freelancer, much of your day could be spent making business calls, going to meetings, and filling out invoices. Molly Owens, founder and owner of Truity.com writes: "Creative careers are less about being (a great artist, a good writer) and more about doing (the processes, routines and endless drafts required to deliver the finished product)."[5]

Here's a final thought for those of you who consider yourself as a creative person: the artistic occupations classified according to Holland's types are not the only occupations that involve creativity in the workplace. According to Carol Eikleberry, PhD, a person can be creative in any field. In her book, *The Career Guide for Creative and Unconventional People*, she writes, "Artistic occupations are simply the ones that provide the best outlet for creative self-expression. Science and engineering provide the best outlet for a different, more objective, kind of creativity."[6]

Hopefully, you will be able to use your creativity to think out of the box and imagine a way to find a career and work environment that best utilizes your talents and fits your personality type.

The following are descriptions of some of the most popular careers for artists:

Animator. Traditional animation involved rapidly showing a series of pictures that were slightly different from each to give the illusion of motion. Today, animation is generated digitally on a computer using special software programs. Animators create animation and visual effects for television, movies, video games, and other forms of media. A bachelor's degree in computer graphics, computer animation, art, or a related field is preferred.

Fashion designer. Fashion designers design clothing and accessories. Because they create their own unique line of clothing and accessories, they need to be on the cutting edge of the latest fashion trends as well as possess sewing and patternmaking skills and a working knowledge of color and textiles. Many fashion designers now use computer-aided design (CAD) programs to create their designs, rather than sketch them out by hand. Fashion design is a highly competitive field and may be stressful. Most people find that a fine arts degree in fashion from a prestigious school is the best preparation.

Graphic artist. Graphic artists translate the client's ideas into a visual representation. Graphic artists may work independently, or they may work for a graphic design firm publication, a publishing company, or an art or marketing department within a company. An associate degree in graphic design is required for assistant or technical support positions; however, most graphic design positions require at least a bachelor's degree.

Illustrator. Like a commercial artist, an illustrator is given guidelines and specification by an art director but has some creative freedom in what the finished work will look like. Illustrators often work on a freelance basis for book and magazine publishers and advertising agencies. Technical illustrators must be knowledgeable in areas such as science, mapmaking, the biological sciences, machinery, engineering, and the solar system. Medical illustrators create visual materials for educational, research, and clinical purposes. They require specialized training—an undergraduate degree in art and science followed by a master's degree in medical illustration.

Interior designer. Interior designers work with fabrics, paint, wallpaper, lighting, furnishings, floor coverings, and accessories to design interior spaces. Interior designers work in both residential and commercial arenas—they may design living rooms, a whole house, hotel lobbies, or executive offices. A bachelor's degree in interior design is required for professional licensure or certification in most states.

Photographer. Photography is a broad field with many specialties such as photography for publication, studio or portrait photography, nature photography, wedding photography, and art photography. Basic and advanced photography skills are essential as well as some basic business and people skills to work with clients.

Set designer. A set designer designs and supervises the construction of sets for the theater. The set designer must be familiar with a wide variety of theatrical styles and artist media while being mindful of budget limits and the physical requirements of the actors.[7] A bachelor's degree in art, design, or theater is recommended, as well as a master of fine arts in theater.

Table 7.1   Jobs in Art

Art and Design	
Advertising artist	Advertising director
Animator	Architect
Fashion designer	Graphic artist
Illustrator	Interior designer
Jewelry designer	Packaging designer
Photographer	Printmaker
Production designer	Set designer
Textile designer	Web designer
Museums	
Curator	Conservator
Curator of education	Customer service manager
Department assistant	Department manager
Docent coordinator	Educator
Exhibit designer	Grants officer
Head of education	Head of public programming
Librarian	Membership officer
Preparator	Public relations officer
Registrar	
Art-Related Businesses	
Artist agent	Art consultant
Art appraiser	Art supply store manager
Corporate curator	Print publisher
Art Galleries	
Archivist	Business manager
Gallery director	Preparator

(Continued)

Education	
Art history instructor	Art school director
Art teacher	Art therapist

Funding Agencies for the Arts	
Assistant program coordinator	Assistant program specialist
Deputy director for budget and administration	Deputy director for programming
Executive director	Program coordinator
Program specialist	Public information officer

Art Journalism	
Assistant editor	Contributing editor
Critic	Designer
Editor	Managing editor
Production assistant	Translator

Auction Galleries	
Customer service manager	Gallery director
Information coordinator	Publicist

It is true that people who major in art or the creative fields may have a more difficult time making a living. Many career areas are very competitive and underpaid. Personal contacts, perseverance, and experience help. Business-related art careers are more plentiful, especially if you can utilize the Internet to advertise your services or sell your work.

Multimedia artists, who provide special effects for film, television, computer graphics, and mobile technology, typically earn an average salary of $58,000.[8] Fashion designers earn slightly more—$61,635 on average, according to Payscale.com.[9] And if you work your way up to a position like a creative art director, your salary could reach over $155,000 per year.[10] The average annual salary range for a medical illustrator is $62,000 to $85,000.[11]

Careers in the Film Industry

People come into the film industry from a variety of backgrounds. One of the most well-known directors, Steven Spielberg, was an amateur filmmaker as a child. Later he dropped out of college and got a job around the set of Universal Studios, thanks to connections from a family friend. He continued to hang around the studio until the executives finally reviewed his short Amblin, which landed a seven-year contract and the beginning of his film career.[12] Even though Spike Lee earned a student academy award at New York University, it did not pay the bills and he worked for a movie distribution house, cleaning and shipping film before he made it as a director.[13]

Even if you're not destined to be the next great screenwriter, there are other ways to gain entry into the film industry such as working behind the scenes as a production assistant, set designer, camera operator, or sound mixer. Networking, perseverance, and being involved in the film-making process any way that you can will eventually pay off.

Table 7.2   Jobs in the Film Industry

Script	
Literary agent	Screenwriter
Script reader	Story editor

Talent	
Animal trainer	Casting director
Choreographer	Extras
Principal actors	Stunt coordinator
Stunt person	Talent agent

Production	
Development executive	Executive producer
Head of production	Line producer
Producer	Production assistant
Production coordinator	Unit production manager

Directing	
DGA trainee	Director
First assistant director	Second assistant director
Script supervisor	

Camera	
Best boy	Camera operator
Director of photography	First assistant cameraperson
Gaffer	Key grip

(Continued)

Education

Acting teacher	Dialect coach
Film instructor	Theater professor

Film Appearance

Art director	Costume designer
Hairstylist/makeup artist	Key costumer
Location scout	Matte painter
Model and miniature builder	Production designer
Puppeteer/sculptor/animatronics	Set designer
Special effects/optical effects	Visual effects producer

Sound

Boom operator	Foley artist
Sound designer	Sound mixer
Supervising sound editor	

Editing

Color timer	Editor

Publicity

Advertising/marketing executive	Entertainment writer
Festival organizer	Film critic
Publicist	Still photographer

Salaries will depend on whether you work for a union or nonunion film. On some low or no budget films, you may not receive anything other than the experience of working on a movie. Indeed.com lists script supervisors in New York as earning an average of $54,000 per year, while script supervisors in Los Angeles earn $42,000 per year.[14]

The median annual salary of a camera operator in the television and motion picture industry is around $77,000, with a range of $64,000 to $97,000.[15]

Careers for Musicians

Whatever music means to you, one thing is for certain—it's a multimillion dollar industry. Although many people hope to be the next Taylor Swift, others will contribute to the music scene by writing songs, composing music, teaching others to sing or dance, or managing the careers of others.

The following are brief descriptions of some nonperformance careers that can be found in the music industry.

A&R coordinator. An artist and repertoire (A&R) coordinator oversees the process of scouting talent and developing artists. An A&R representative signs and develops talent for a record label. The A&R coordinator oversees the entire musical project. Many employees start off as interns or in another sector of the music industry before moving up to an A&R administrator, A&R scout, or A&R coordinator.[16] Record labels like to see employees who have experience in the music industry plus backgrounds in business, communications, or marketing.

Recording engineer. Recording engineers shape the sound of an album by recording, editing, and mixing sound. They use a variety of recording technology from analog tape to digital multitrack recording programs. According to Careers in Music.com, "In many studios, the Recording Engineer is also the Producer, overseeing both artistic and technical elements of the recording session."[17] "Recording Engineers often start as Runners before moving on to become Assistant Engineers and finally becoming Engineers. Advancement can come in the form of working with celebrity clients, working at a famous studio, or running their own personal recording studio."[18]

Although there are no educational requirements to become a recording engineer, it is a definite advantage to earn a degree in audio engineering from a technical or trade school, community college, or four-year university.

Sound technician. The sound technician is an important part of an artist's performance. Sound technicians use the soundboard and other audio equipment to ensure correct sound levels and mixing. Some sound technicians also assist with lighting and special effects. Long hours and late nights are a part of the job. Networking and building relationships is an important part of finding employment in this field.

There is no required degree to become a sound technician. A degree in music production, music technology, or audio engineering from a technical school or community college can help you learn the basics. Getting practical experience is critical, so try to acquire as much experience as you can—paid or volunteer.

Salaries in the music industry vary greatly and will depend on how big a company is, where it is located, and the applicant's talent and experience. Sound technicians and recording engineers can start at $20,000 to $25,000 and may make up to $50,000 plus yearly. Higher salaries will go to sound technicians who go on the road with well-known acts. A&R

Table 7.3   Jobs in the Music Industry

Recording Industry

A&R coordinator/director	A&R administrator
Arranger	Artist relations and development
Copyist	Director of publicity
Field merchandiser	Label representative
Licensing representative	Marketing representative
Orchestrator	Promotion manager
Regional sales manager	Record producer
Recording engineer	Staff publicist

Radio and Television

Disc jockey	Music director
Program director	

On the Road

Advance person	Road manager
Sound technician	Tour coordinator
Tour publicist	

Arenas, Facilities, Halls, and Clubs

Concert hall manager	Nightclub manager
Resident sound technician	

Education

College or conservatory teacher	Music librarian
Music therapist	Private, public school teacher
Private instrument/voice teacher	

Music Retailing and Wholesaling

Instrument sales representative	Music/record shop manager

The Business End of the Industry

Booking agent	Business manager
Concert promoter	Music publisher
Professional manager	

Repair, Restoration, and Design

Bow rehairer and restorer	Instrument repair and restoration
Musical instrument building/designer	Piano tuner-technician

(Continued)

Table 7.3 (Continued)

Publicity

Music journalist	Publicist/assistant publicist

Symphonies, Orchestras, Operas

Business manager	Concertmaster/concertmistress
Conductor	Director of development
Director of educational activities	Managing director
Personnel director	Public relations
Opera singer	Orchestra manager
Orchestral music librarian	Section leader/member
Subscriptions and ticket service director	

Talent and Writing

Background vocalist	Dance band
Floor show group	Recording group
Session musician	Songwriter

coordinators can reach as high as $85,000 plus and even more from signing bonuses for acquiring "superstar" talent.[19] Major record producers can make well over $1,000,000 if they can sign on top recording stars.

Careers for Writers

Writers create written content for advertising and marketing, books, magazines and trade journals, newspapers, online publications, company newsletters, movie and television scripts, radio and television broadcasts, songs, blogs, and other types of media. Technology and market changes have propelled the print industry into the digital age, creating new opportunities for writers and journalists with digital newspapers and magazines, wire services, and websites. The emergence of social media has also changed the face of journalism. Facebook, Twitter, and LinkedIn now serve as news sources for many of their followers.

There are several career options available for writers. Here are some examples:

Copy writer. Copy writers can find employment in the business world: a copywriter for an advertising company, an editor for a book or magazine publisher, or a member of the public relations team of a major corporation writing press releases and newsletters. Copywriters can also find employment in the video game, movie, and broadcasting industries.

Editor. Editors oversee the publication production, including artwork, layout, typesetting, printing, and release of a project. They read, review, make recommendations, and work with writers to refine and move the project along to completion. Depending on the employer, editors must work within the deadlines and resources of the company. A nonfiction editor may spend six months to a year collaborating with the author, while a newspaper editor may have only minutes or a few hours to check or rework a story. Editors can find employment in many fields such as film, video, magazine, newspaper, blog, and book publishing, both fiction and nonfiction.

Freelance writer. Freelance writers are self-employed writers who write and sell their work to newspapers, publishers, manufacturers, public relations departments, advertising agencies, and the media. They can also write for social media, websites, or blogs. Creative agencies employ both full-time and freelance writers.[20]

Ghostwriter. Ghostwriting is a special kind of writing because they write the copy and receive paycheck but receive no recognition beyond that. Movie stars and other famous personalities often hire ghostwriters to write their memoirs. Ghostwriting is also a common practice in politics, business, and the entertainment industry.

Proofreader. Proofreaders read copy to detect and correct errors. They are considered essential to authors, publishers, and editorial boards. Proofreaders are expected to be accurate, especially in the publishing industry, because they are the last stage of the publication process. Proofreaders must possess a firm understanding of grammar and spelling, have an eye for detail, and be a perfectionist.

Scriptwriter. All of your favorite sitcoms employ a team of scriptwriters. Scriptwriters or screenwriters write the scripts that films, television programs, comics, commercials, or video games are based. Television script writers must meet the needs of specific time slots, audiences, and series parameters. When writing plays, a script writer must consider the limited staging area and the fact that most of the story is told in dialog.

Speechwriters. Rarely do the top executives of any organization write their own speeches. They often hire professional speech writers. Speech writers must be skilled in understanding both their audience and the speaker. Speechwriters can be freelancers, work for an agency, or be employed full time by the company.

Technical writer. Technical writing differs from creative or nonfiction writing because it requires communicating complex information in a concise and accurate manner. Technical writers develop user guides, reference manuals, installation guides, and service manuals for a wide range of household products. They also write training materials, conference presentations, scientific journal articles, and official documentation.

A college degree in English, journalism, or communications is generally required for a full-time position as a writer, journalist, or author. Experience can be gained through internships, but any form of writing that can improve your skill, such as blogging, is beneficial.

If you have excellent writing skills, there are many writing opportunities for you as a writer. Many creative fiction writers find it useful to join local writers' groups for support and feedback on their work. To gain exposure, enter poetry or short story competitions or blog or develop your own website.

In the publishing industry, big-name authors like J. K. Rowling and James Patterson earn millions of dollars in royalties each year. Most

Table 7.4   Jobs for Writers

Newspapers and News Services

Assistant editor	Columnist
Copy aide	Copyeditor
Critic general assignment reporter	Editorial writer
Financial wire reporter	News editor
News librarian	Reporter specialist
Section editor	Wire service reporter

Magazines

Associate editor	Circulation director
Copyeditor	Editor
Editorial assistant	Executive editor
News librarian	Researcher
Senior editor	

Television

Anchor	Assistant news director
Community-affairs director	Desk assistant
News director	News librarian
News writer	Reporter
Researcher	

(Continued)

Scholastic, Academic, and Nonprofit

Alumni communications specialist	Alumni magazine editor
Assistant professor	Journalism teacher
Librarian	News director
Professor	Social media manager
Web content writer/editor	

Book Publishing

Assistant editor	Associate editor
Copyeditor	Copywriter
Editor	Editorial assistant
Electronic publishing product manager	Literary agent
Publicity manager	Promotion manager
Promotional assistant—electronic publishing	Proof reader
Researcher	Technical writer
Senior editor	

Arts and Entertainment

Author	Greeting card writer
Ghostwriter/collaborator	Lyricist/jingle writer
Playwright	Poet
Scriptwriter/screenwriter	

Business Communication

Communications coordinator	External publications editor
Government affairs specialist	Internal publications editor
Public information officer	Public relations account executive
Public relations assistant	Social media manager
Speechwriter	Technical communicator

Advertising

Account executive	Assistant copywriter
Copywriter	Social media manager

Federal Government

Editorial assistant and clerk	Political speechwriter
Press secretary	Technical writer and editor
Writer and editor	

authors, however, earn a more modest income. The average income for an editor is around $49,000 across the industry.[21] According to Payscale .com, commissions constitute a fair portion (just over two-fifths) of the income for editors. Professional speechwriters, like those who write speeches for political candidates, can earn $101,000 to $157,000, but those salaries can vary greatly.[22]

Careers in Theater

If you have a love for drama, acting, and the production of theater in general, then theater may be the career for you. However, not all theater

Table 7.5   Jobs in Theater

Performance	
Actor/actress	
Production, Directing, Design	
Assistant casting director	Assistant scenic designer
Casting director	Costume designer
Director	Lighting designer
Producer	Production assistant
Scenic designer	Sound designer
Stage manager	
Theatrical Administration	
Company manager	Box office treasurer
Press agent	Press agent apprentice
Behind the Scenes	
Lighting person	Makeup artist
Production hairstylist	Sound technician
Star dresser	Wardrobe dresser
Education	
Drama coach	Theater arts professor
Miscellaneous	
Advance person	Arts council director
Fund-raiser	

majors need to act. There are many other aspects of theater such as lighting, staging, or writing. You could also be a stage manager or a booking agent or teach theater or drama in high school or at a university.

Job opportunities can be found in community theaters, school theaters, opera houses, and performing arts centers. Some even work for traveling theater troupes. Theater majors also go on to have successful careers in the arts, business, education, government, performance, and publishing.

A Broadway actor's salary is determined by the actors' union, Actors' Equity Association. As Olivia Rubino-Finn explains in her article, "The Bare Minimum: Breaking down Broadway Actor Salaries," "The whole of Broadway operates under a universal agreement negotiated by Equity that lays down practically every rule of operation under the sun, just as off-Broadway, regional theatres, readings, and tours have their own specific agreements to which they must adhere."[23]

According to Indeed.com, the average salary of a Broadway actor in New York was $55,000 in 2016.[24]

CHAPTER EIGHT

Careers for People Who Are Hands-On

He who has a why can endure any how.

—Nietzsche

How Do I Know If I'm Hands-On?

People who are hands-on usually like being outdoors, playing sports, or working with plants or animals. They may enjoy building, woodworking, and working with tools. Most hands-on people do not enjoy working with people as much as they like working with things. They are practical and no-nonsense and like to see a result of their efforts.

Hands-on people often choose careers in mechanics, construction, manufacturing, law enforcement, athletics, animals, the military, and the skilled trades. If you like to work with your hands you may want to be a jeweler designer or a mechanic. Auto mechanics like to work on cars and keep them in perfect running order. CNC operators shape huge sheets of metal or plastic, and crane operators maneuver construction material. Other examples of hands-on occupations are welders, robotic tech electricians, plumbers, maintenance technicians, carpenters, computer repairers, florists, massage therapists, cosmetologists, dental hygienists, surgeons, physical therapists, vet techs, chefs, fitness trainers, drafters, glassblowers, and sculptors. Right now skilled workers in manufacturing are in hot demand.

Community colleges and technical schools offer one-year certifications, associate degrees, and even bachelor degrees in these majors.

Table 8.1   List of Careers That Are Considered Primarily Hands-On

• Animal breeder or trainer	• Artesian or craftsperson
• Athlete	• Auto mechanic
• Building inspector	• Camera operator or film editor
• Cardiovascular technologist	• Carpenter
• Coach	• Computer support
• Construction	• Culinary or food preparation
• Drafting	• Electrician
• Engineering, engineering technology	• Farmer (animals, fruits, vegetables)
• Fire fighter	• Forester
• Heating, plumbing, air conditioning	• Heavy equipment operator
• Landscaping/nursery owner	• Machinist
• Manufacturing	• Medical technology
• Nurse aid	• Pilot
• Police officer or detective	• Power plant operator
• Printing	• Radiologic technologist
• Surgical technologist	• Surveying, surveying technology
• Truck driver	• Veterinary technician

Four-year colleges offer baccalaureate degrees in engineering and engineering technology (including surveying engineering).

Working with Animals

Who hasn't dreamed of working with puppies and kittens all day or reintroducing wildlife back into the woods? While your first thought may be the popular field of veterinary medicine, there are many other animal careers that may be of interest to you such as becoming an animal behaviorist. Animal behaviorists generally have a background in biology, psychology, zoology, or animal science or have extensive experience working with or training animals. Jackson Galaxy, cat behaviorist, author, and the host of Animal Planet's hit show *My Cat From Hell* has a master's degree in theater arts and writes and plays music when he's not working with cats. He began his cat behaviorist career working at the Humane Society of Boulder Valley.[1] Cesar Millan, another best-selling author and speaker, got his start in the United States as a dog groomer. He later started a freelance dog rehabilitation service that eventually led to opening his first Dog Psychology Center.[2]

Table 8.2   Jobs for Those Who Love to Work with Animals

Veterinary Careers

Veterinarian	Veterinary nurse
Veterinary technician	

Breeding and Farming

Agricultural extension agent	Animal breeder or farmer
Animal health inspector	Artificial insemination technician
Livestock judge	Meat inspector

Careers with Birds

Exotic bird breeder	Poultry farmer
Ornithologist	

Careers with Dogs and Cats

Animal control officer	Animal cruelty investigator
Animal shelter manager	Dog breeder
Dog groomer	Dog trainer
K-9 police officer	Pet adoption counselor

Wildlife Careers

Fish and game management	Wildlife biologist
Wildlife educator	Wildlife rehabilitator
Wildlife veterinarian	Zoologist

Other Animal Health Careers

Animal behaviorist	Animal geneticist
Animal massage therapist	Animal nutritionist
Animal scientist	Lab animal technician

Careers with Horses

Barn manager	Bloodstock agent
Broodmare manager	Exercise rider/groom
Farrier	Foaling attendant
Horse show judge	Horse trainer

Careers with Marine Animals

Aquarist	Ichthyologist
Marine biologist	Marine mammal trainer

(Continued)

Table 8.2   (Continued)

Careers with Reptiles	
Herpetologist	Reptile breeder

Other Animal Careers	
Animal science/poultry professor	Movie animal trainer
Nature/pet writer	Pet portrait artist
Pet/wildlife photographer	

There is a wide range in pay in the animal care industry. Veterinarians and researchers/educators tend to earn the most pay, while many animal care and service positions earn less than $30,000 a year. According to the American Veterinary Medical Association, "Starting salaries for new veterinarians have begun to recover from the economic downturn of 2008 through 2012."[3] The starting salary for all veterinary students in 2014 was $51,917.[4] Those who accepted a full-time position in private practice made almost $15,000 more. The AVMA report also noted that female veterinarians earned a starting salary of $2,438 *less* than male veterinarians.[5]

The average salary for a wildlife biologist is $56,000.[6] A horse trainer earns an average salary just over $30,000 per year (experience strongly influences the pay for this job).[7]

The Automotive Industry

The auto industry is quickly evolving, and there are plenty of opportunities for individuals who love to fix, design, manufacture, or race automobiles.

Job opportunities are plentiful in the auto industry—currently there is a severe shortage of auto techs nationwide. Employment can be found at independent garages, automotive service chains, car dealerships, automotive supply stores, and parts departments, and with companies that sell retail, wholesale or online automotive parts, aftermarket parts, and supplies.

The salary for an entry-level automotive mechanic is about $36,000, with a range of $32,000 to $42,000.[8]

Tractor trailer truck drivers make an average salary of almost $49,000, with a range of $43,000 to $56,000.[9] An auto parts dealer's salary averages $52,000, and a parts and service manager can make an average salary of $78,000.[10]

Table 8.3   Jobs in the Automotive Industry

Design and Production	
Assembler/fabricator	Automotive designer
Automotive painter/detailer	CNC operator
Machinist	Mechanical engineer

Repair and Restoration	
Air-conditioning technician	Alignment technician
Auto body repair technician	Automotive glass installer
Automotive painter	Auto upholsterer
Brake specialist	Branch manager
Diesel mechanic	Emission control specialist
Service manager	Service technician/mechanic
Tire repairer	Tune-up technician

Racing	
Crew chief	Design engineer
Pit crew	Race car driver
Race car team mechanic	Racing school instructor

Sales	
Auto body customizer	Automotive franchise owner
Automotive technician	Detailer
Finance/insurance manager	General manager
New and used car salesperson	Service manager
Service writer	

Other Automotive Careers	
Auto claims adjuster/appraiser	Automotive instructor
Automotive museum director	Automotive parts/sales manager
Driving instructor	Manufacturer's representative
Motorcycle mechanic	Motorboat mechanic

Students who wish to continue their education beyond a community college or technical school can transfer to four-year colleges for engineering or marketing/sales. Motor sports enthusiasts are employed by race teams locally or all over the country. Salary depends on the team and its racing success.

Criminal Justice

If you are interested in working in the public sector and making a difference in your community, there are a variety of career pathways available in criminal justice. Criminal justice careers include subfields such as law enforcement, corrections, forensic science, criminology, homeland security, private security, academia, and legal services. Some of the positions in criminal justice such as becoming a police officer can be stressful and dangerous. Officers put themselves in harm's way on a daily basis to protect the general public and respond to emergency calls.

The following are brief descriptions of career opportunities in the field of criminal justice:

Law enforcement. Law enforcement encompasses city, county, or state police office; security officers; and federal law enforcement agents. Police officers are the first line of defense against crime. The minimum requirements to become a police officer are a high school degree or GED and passing scores on written and physical evaluations. However, an associate degree or bachelor's degree in criminal justice-related degree can significantly increase your career options. Often a degree is required for jobs at the state level or to advance to a detective or police leadership position.

Federal law enforcement agents prevent and investigate crime. They work directly for a particular government agency such as the FBI, DEA, IRS, INS, Department of Homeland Security, or Secret Service. Federal law enforcement jobs are highly selective and select only top-quality candidates. A college degree is usually required.

Crime scene investigation. Crime scene investigators document crime scenes and collect physical evidence. Crime scene investigators are trained in how to properly gather fingerprints, DNA samples, and other evidence for analysis and admittance in a court of law. An associate degree is the minimum requirement for some evidence and documentation positions, but a bachelor's or master's degree may be required to work in a crime laboratory.

Corrections officers. Corrections careers involve securing inmates in jails and prison, conducting routine inspections, providing reports on inmate behavior, and enforcing the rule of the facility. Although the minimum requirements for a correction position is a high school diploma or GED, you will have a much better chance of being promoted and earning a higher salary, if you have a college degree.

Probation and parole officers. Probation officers supervise criminals who have been sentenced to probation rather than serving time in jail. Juvenile probation officers work with juveniles who have been sentenced to probation. According to the Juvenile Probation Officer Career Guide, "Juvenile probation officers conduct regular visits to the juvenile's home, school, work, and other areas of the community which the juvenile frequents. The visits may be weekly or monthly depending on the level of supervision imposed by the court."[11]

Parole officers supervise offenders after they are released from prison, usually from an early release. Both types of officers help the newly released offender make lifestyle choices that will prevent a return trip to prison. Parole officers may also help the offender secure employment and may travel to various locations within the state. A bachelor's degree is required by most states, but experience and an advanced degree, such as a master's degree, may be required to advance to supervisor or administrative positions.

Table 8.4   Jobs in Criminal Justice

Local Law Enforcement	
City or county police	Juvenile Justice Center Staff
Park police	Sheriff Department

State Law Enforcement	
Attorney general	Corrections officer
Liquor control board officer	Narcotics bureaus staff
State crime lab technicians	State police

Private Sector Law Enforcement	
Private detective	Safety officer
Security patrol officer	

Federal Law Enforcement	
Customs officer	Department of Defense
Department of Homeland Security	Department of Transportation
Federal Bureau of Investigation	Federal Trade Commission
Food and Drug Administration	Immigration and Naturalization
The inspector general	Veterans Affairs

Judicial System	
Bailiff	Detention center staff
District attorney	Judge
Lawyer	Probation officer

According to Monster.com, "Those starting out in entry-level jobs and lacking a college degree can expect to make about $25,000 a year. Those holding bachelor's degrees can expect to make nearly double that."[12] Individuals with specialized degrees or extensive experience can make between $70,000 and $166,000 a year. In general, average annual salaries in law enforcement range from the lowest paid security guard at $29,000 to a police officer at $53,000 to a police chief at $102,000.[13] Positions at the state and federal levels earn higher salaries.

Hospitality

In the past, working in the food industry typically meant becoming a cook or restaurant chef. But today, the culinary industry offers a wide range of opportunities such as food television, cookbook publishing, owning and operating a restaurant, and creating unique pastry products.[14]

According to the Institute of Culinary Education, "Catering is one of the largest segments of the food industry. From elaborate seated wedding dinners to prepared lunch sandwich platters, catered food is constantly in demand."[15] For those who think they would enjoy managing special events, positions can be found with catering and event companies, and at hotels, resorts, museums, universities, and restaurant groups.[16]

"Opportunities also abound in the world of digital food media, due to the popularity of video content on such sites as Tasting Table or Food52. Food photography and styling are also in high demand, as the market for visual food content has grown with the popularity of such sites as Instagram and Pinterest."[17] Food stylists prepare the food and then "stage" it for its media debut in magazines, newspapers, books, television, and advertisements. An artistic eye as well as the ability to cook is needed to have a successful career as a food stylist.[18]

Nutritionists are another culinary-related occupation. Instead of focusing on creating food dishes, nutritionists combine cooking and science to study how the human body metabolizes the specific nutrients in food. Most nutritionists hold at least a bachelor's degree.[19] A registered dietician must have a bachelor's degree plus a license to practice in the field. Nutritionists and dieticians can find employment at hospitals, nursing homes, and cafeterias; have private consultation practices; or work for magazines and television shows.

Another science-based side of a culinary arts degree is food science. Food science focuses on the physical and chemical aspects of food. It is food scientists who develop new foods and better ways of preserving and processing our food. When I was in college, one of my roommates was a food science major. One summer she did an internship at the Pillsbury

Company in Minneapolis and worked on developing a new line of frosting flavors.

Food scientists typically work for food manufacturers or university laboratories and research facilities. At large universities, the food science major can be found in the College of Agriculture.

Chefs and head cooks make an average of $41,610, bakers make an average of $23,600, and food service managers make an average of $48,560.[20] For the latest salary information, visit All Culinary Schools at http://www.allculinaryschools.com.

Table 8.5   Jobs in the Hospitality Industry

Catering/Deli/Take-Out

Catering cook	Caterer
Catering operations manager	Deli/fast-food store manager
Deli prep and clean-up person	Party planner

Restaurants

Chef	Cooks
Dining room manager	Host/hostess
Kitchen steward	Pastry chef
Sous-chef	Bakery manager
Bread baker	

Gourmet Foods and Groceries

Farmers market manager	Restaurant supply buyer
Restaurant supply salesperson	Specialty food store buyer/manager

Culinary Schools and Training

Culinary school director	Culinary/pastry arts teacher

Nutrition and Dietetics

Nutritionist	Registered dietician
University nutrition instructor	Residence dietitian
Sports nutritionist	

Hotel

Concierge	Desk clerk
General manager	Front office manager
Reservations manager	Sales manager

(Continued)

Table 8.5   (Continued)

Institutional Food	
Hotel catering manager	Hotel executive chef
Hotel food and beverage manager	Institutional chef
Institutional head cook	Servers

Specialty Food Products	
Candy maker	Cheese maker
Plant operations manager	Quality control manager
Sausage and ham producer	Savory and Sweet Condiments Maker
State agriculture marketing advisor	Winery cellar master
Winery chemist, winemaker	Winery publicist
Winery sales manager	Winery tasting room manager

Writing and Publishing	
Cookbook author	Cookbook editor/publisher
Food editor/director	Food critic/writer
Food historian	Food photographer
Food researcher	Food stylist
Recipe developer/tester	

Tourism	
Cruise ship chef/staff	Meeting planner
Resort manager	Tour guide
Travel agent	Visitor's bureau director

The Sports Industry

Not all careers in the sports industry involve becoming a professional athlete. If you're interested in the world of sports and athletics but prefer to be off the field (or court), there are plenty of alternatives. If you're interested in the business side of the sports industry, you could major in sports management. If you love working with kids, you could become a coach. If you enjoy the health-care field, you could become an athletic trainer or a physical therapist. If you like to talk or write about sporting events, then think about becoming a sports reporter or a sports announcer.

There is a wide range of salaries in the sport industry. It's no surprise that the highest salaries are awarded to professional athletes, who can

Table 8.6   Jobs in the Sports Industry

Professional Athletes

LPGA tour player	Professional baseball player
Professional basketball player	Professional women's basketball player
Professional football player	Professional hockey player
Professional boxer	Professional soccer player

Professional Sports Teams

Business manager	Cheerleader
Director of baseball operations	Director of minor league operations
Equipment manager	Marketing assistant
Marketing director	Professional scout
Promotion director	Publicist
Public relations director	Team general manager

Sports Business and Administration

Athletic program development director	Account executive for special-risk insurance
Professional sports agent	Sports event coordinator
Sports industry publicist	Sports facility manager
Sports information director (college)	Sports statistician

Wholesaling and Retailing

Manufacturer's representative	Sporting goods manager

Coaching and Education

Athletic director	Coach (High School, College)
Manager (professional sports team)	Physical education instructor

Sports Officiating

Pro baseball umpire	Amateur/scholastic baseball umpire
Pro football referee	Amateur/scholastic football referee
Amateur/scholastic basketball referee	Other sports referee

Sports Journalism

Sportswriter	Sports columnist
Television/radio sportscaster	Sports photographer

(*Continued*)

Table 8.6 (Continued)

Recreation and Fitness	
Aerobics instructor	Health club assistant manager
Health club manager	Golf, tennis pro
Personal trainer	Sports and fitness program coordinator

Sports Medicine	
Athletic trainer	Physical therapist, assistant
Sports and fitness nutritionist	Sports physician

earn hundreds of millions of dollars for a multiyear contract. But the odds of becoming drafted by the NFL are extremely low. According to the NCAA's own statistics, only 1.6 percent of NCAA football players made it into the NFL. Baseball players fared a little better at 9.7 percent.[21] Athletic coaches can expect a modest salary average of $40,000, but head football coaches at the college level can earn $250,000 to several million dollars at big name universities. The median annual salary for an athletic trainer is around $42,500, with a range of $39,000 to $48,000.[22]

CHAPTER NINE

Careers for Organizers

Success is not the key to happiness. Happiness is the key to success.
If you love what you are doing, you will be successful.
—Albert Schweitzer

How Do I Know If I'm an Organizer?

If you are an organizer, you will probably like completing orderly, well-defined tasks in a structured environment. You may enjoy working with numbers, data, and files. You probably value accuracy and precision, like to get things done, and take care of every detail. You prefer to carry out tasks initiated by others, rather than being in a position of authority.

Most organizers dislike unstructured work environments that lack clear expectations and procedures. They like to work through tasks in a methodical, systematized manner and do not want to have to make things up as they go. Most organizers like to work with data, information, and files.

Business

The field of business is so broad that it encompasses every aspect of the way we do business in our country. Depending on their specialty, a business major may be involved in accounting, marketing, finance, economics, management, logistics, information processing, human resources, sales, or real estate. They may work for a company, lead a company, or create their own company.

An associate degree in business will allow you to move into entry-level jobs such as customer service, sales, human resources clerk, purchasing

Table 9.1   Jobs in Business

Accounting

Accounting clerk	Accountant
Accounts supervisor	Auditor
Bookkeeper	Certified public accountant
Cost accountant	Financial analyst
Forensic accountant	Tax examiner
Tax preparer	Tax specialist

Legal

Court reporter	Legal secretary
Paralegal	

Other

Casino manager	Event/meeting planner
Entrepreneur	Gaming dealer
Inspector	Training specialist

Medical

Billing/coding specialist	Medical receptionist
Medical secretary	Medical transcriptionist

Banking

Accounts manager	Bank manager
Credit analyst	Loan interviewer/specialist

Retail

Manager	Manager trainee
Buyer, purchasing manager	

Corporate/Office

Accounts payable/receivable clerk	Bill collector
Budget analyst	Claims adjuster
Controller	Credit manager
Executive secretary	Human resources manager
Insurance adjuster	Investment consultant
Payroll clerk	Personal financial planner
Purchasing manager	Recruiter
Sales representative	Secretary/administrative assistant
Title examiner	Trainer
Underwriter	

clerk, accounts payable/receivable clerk, insurance agent (with training and certifications), supply chain clerk, and a manager trainee in retail and other service-related industries. However, employers will usually require at least a bachelor's degree for positions in accounting, finance, management, logistics, and operations. The highest-paying occupations within the business industry are the following:

- Business operations (e.g., claims adjusters, benefits specialists, management analysts, and market research analysts)
- Financial specialists (e.g., accountants and auditors, credit analysts, financial examiners, and personal financial advisors)
- Management (e.g., chief executive officers, IT managers, financial managers, human resources managers, marketing and sales managers, health services managers, and purchasing managers)
- Sales (e.g., supervisors, retail and wholesale sales reps, insurance agents, real estate agents, and financial services reps)
- Related business occupations (e.g., actuaries, economists, operations research analysts, industrial-organizational psychologists, statisticians, and public relations specialists)

Here are some things to keep in mind when considering a business occupation. Managers and management analysts may be some of the highest-paid individuals, but they also work longer hours than many other occupations. According to a BLS article by Elka Torpey, "The District of Columbia, Virginia, and Maryland had the highest concentrations of management analysts."[1] Sales positions have some of the lowest starting salaries but have the potential for very high earnings (over $100,000). Sales reps for scientific and technical products have the highest pay, although there are fewer jobs. Ms. Torpey writes, "Jobs for scientific and technical products sales representatives were concentrated in New Hampshire, Massachusetts, and Ohio; those for workers who sell other types of products had high concentrations of jobs in Wisconsin, Michigan, and Georgia."[2]

Accounting

Do you consider yourself to be a "numbers person"?

Do you appreciate predictability?

Do you organize data or information in a sequential manner?

Do you like to analyze and solve puzzles?

If you answered "yes" to these questions, then accounting may be a good career choice for you. Consider taking one or two accounting classes first to assess your interests and abilities.

Today a career in accounting is more than just crunching numbers in a small office cubicle. Computer programs have streamlined many of the processes that some might have considered boring in the past. Modern accountants spend time networking with clients and are an integral part of their business team.

One nice thing about accounting is that you can enter the field at both the associate and bachelor's levels. An associate degree will prepare you for entry-level accounting positions, while a bachelor's degree will prepare you to sit for the certified public accountant (CPA) certification.

Some typical job titles for accounting majors with a bachelor's degree or higher are the following:

Forensic accountant, senior accountant, tax accountant, financial analyst, junior accountant, staff accountant, controller, chief financial officer, tax manager, business analyst, auditor, and director of finance. In addition, self-employment is always an option.

The more common career paths four-year accounting majors have available to them are public, private, government, and forensic accounting.

The more common types of activities in public accounting are auditing, tax preparation, and consulting. The accountant is employed by a certified public accounting firm and works on various clients' information for that firm. People in this career path normally become certified public accountants.

Private accounting is where the accountant works for one company. There are different positions that an accountant can enter in a company. The most common for a four-year degreed student is a supervisory role of the accounting department. This position is usually referred to as the controller. Accountants who work within a company usually focus on budgeting, cash management, monthly financial statements, and guiding the financial decisions of the company.

There are different types of positions available for accounting majors in the government arena. Accountants are needed in the federal, state, and local levels of government. Some agencies an accounting major maybe interested in are the Internal Revenue Service as an auditor, or the Federal Bureau of Investigations as an accountant. There are many options in this area.

Forensic accounting is one of the newest career paths of accounting majors. Forensic accountants are charged with investigating business errors or frauds, reporting on these, as well as preparing and testifying in a court of law on their findings.

According to the BLS, "Employment of accountants and auditors is projected to grow 11 percent from 2014 to 2024, faster than the average for all occupations. In general, employment growth of accountants and auditors is expected to be closely tied to the health of the overall economy. As the economy grows, more workers should be needed to prepare and examine financial records."[3] According to NACE, the average starting salary for accounting majors in 2016 was $52,163.[4]

Visit Careers in Accounting (http://www.accounting.com/careers) for more information about a career in the accounting field.

Actuarial Science

If you have a head for numbers and love statistics, you might excel as an actuary. Actuaries analyze the costs of risk and uncertainty using statistics, mathematics, and financial theory. Most actuaries work for the insurance industry but also hired by the state and federal government, research universities, banks, and even labor unions. Actuaries assess the risk that an event will occur and, based on that, develop policies for businesses and clients to minimize the cost of that risk. To become a certified professional, you will need to pass a series of exams. Actuaries are well compensated—the median annual salary for actuaries is over $97,000 a year, according to the Bureau of Labor Statistics.[5]

Administration and Administrative Support

Office and Administrative Support occupations are employed in almost every type of industry from schools and manufacturing plants to collection agencies, grocery stores, and executive offices. They perform clerical and administrative duties such as answering the phone, scheduling appointments, organizing files, preparing documents, entering data, operating various types of office equipment, and supporting other staff. People in these occupations usually have interests and skills using and manipulating data. They have to have good communication and customer service skills, be able to work as a member of a team, pay close attention to detail, and possess a high level of accuracy.

Legal and medical secretaries usually require additional training beyond high school to learn industry-specific terminology and procedures. Executive secretaries usually need some college training and several years of related work experience. Administrative assistants and secretaries make an average annual salary of $35,500.[6]

Court Reporting and Captioning

Do you have a good grasp of the English language?
Are you a good listener?
Can you type well?
Are you interested in working in the legal field?

If so, then a career in court reporting and captioning may be for you.

Court reporters create word-for-word (real-time) transcriptions at trials, depositions, and other legal proceedings. Some court reporters provide captioning for television and real-time translation or communication access real-time translation (CART) services for hearing-impaired people at public events, in business meetings, or in classrooms. Court reporting uses a system of letters and phrases that allows good stenographers to reach speeds of over 225 words per minute. There are employment opportunities for freelancers, with court reporting companies, or for the court system. Court reporting programs can be found at community and technical colleges. The average salary for a court reporter is $49,500 a year.[7]

For more information about the world of court reporting, visit the National Reporters Association (http://www.ncra.org).

Health Care

Health-care facility administrator. A health-care administrator or manager manages the daily business operations of a health-care facility. A bachelor's degree in health policy and administration is required; a master's degree is preferred. Average annual salary: $50,000 to $170,000.[8]

Medical assistant. Performs routine administrative and clinical duties in a medical, clinical, or health-care facility office. A one-year training program or associate degree is required. Average annual salary: $30,548.[9]

Health Information Management

The Bureau of Labor Statistics predicts that, "Employment of health information technicians is projected to grow 15 percent from 2014 to 2024, much faster than the average for all occupations. The demand for health services is expected to increase as the population ages."[10]

Medical billing and coding. Medical billers process invoices, collect payment, and follow up on claims sent to health insurance companies for reimbursement of services rendered by a health-care provider. Medical coding professionals ensure that medical and diagnostic codes are applied correctly during the medical billing process. Medical coding professionals who want to increase their earnings or become freelance coders should have an associate degree and obtain the certified professional coder (CPC) credential.

Average annual salary: $35,000 to $50,000.[11] Credentialed coders can earn substantially more based on experience and specialty (averaging almost $55,000).[12]

For more information about becoming a medical biller or coder, read the "What Is Medical Coding?" article located at https://www.aapc.com /medical-coding/medical-coding.aspx.

Medical records technician and administrator. Like paralegals, medical records managers and technicians do a lot of solitary organization work. They plan, design, secure, and manage data; organize patient information; and maintain patients' medical histories for hospitals and physicians' offices. An associate degree in medical administration is required for technicians, but a bachelor's degree in health information management is needed for management positions. Average annual salary for administrators: $63,382 to $88,767.[13]

Medical scribe. A medical scribe inputs patient data (e.g., history or symptoms), records examination results, and prepares charts. Recently, the federal government mandated that health-care facilities and providers use electronic medical records (EMRs). As a result, doctors have begun using medical scribes to help them become more efficient. Education for a scribe is often on-the-job training or a one-year training program at a community college or vocational school. Average wage: $11.99 per hour.[14]

Medical transcription. Medical transcriptionists, also known as professionally trained health-care documentation specialists, have evolved as a profession. The early medical transcriptionists were responsible only for copying the notes written by physicians into patient records. However, soon the job evolved into taking doctor dictations in shorthand. With the advent of speech recognition software, many thought that medical transcriptionists would be history, but instead the industry reinvented itself. Now instead of tedious typists, medical transcription requires skilled professionals who can edit computer-generated health-care reports for quality and accuracy.[15]

Less than one year of training is required, but an associate degree is preferred. Median annual salary: $38,487 to $48,156.[16]

Human Resources

Human resources clerk. Human resources assistants and clerks help maintain employee records. They may perform general clerical duties, such as answering the phone, or may assist in other areas, such as hiring and orienting new workers. They need to be organized, work well with others, and be able to keep information confidential. At least an associate degree is preferred. The median annual human resources assistant I salary is around $38,000, with a range of $34,000 to $43,000.[17]

Human resources manager. Human resources managers are responsible for maintaining good working relationships between employers and employees. They have a wide range of responsibilities, which include overseeing hiring, benefits, salaries, and employee training; answering questions about company health plan and benefits; helping coworkers settle disagreements; and making sure that supervisors and managers treat employees fairly. A human resources manager should be able to communicate clearly, maintain confidentiality and equity, and enjoy working with all types of people. A bachelor's degree is required; master's degree is often preferred for top-level positions. The median annual human resources manager's salary in 2016 was around $95,000, with a range of $83,000 to $107,500 according to Salary.com.[18]

Library Science

Although the types of materials on library shelves have basically remained unchanged over the years, the nature of library services has been profoundly altered by the onset of modern technology.[19] Librarians have evolved into information specialists who help their patrons locate information on the Internet, via digital databases, and through virtual and remote access.

In general, librarians oversee libraries and help patrons find information. They also acquire, preserve, and catalog information and handle archives. Librarians can specialize in a particular area such as medicine, law, government, fine art, rare books, music, maps, and film/video. In colleges and universities librarians often teach information literacy to students: how to find, evaluate, and use information from print and online sources. At public libraries librarians often work with and provide programs for specific groups of people such as children, senior citizens, the unemployed, prisoners, the homeless, and visually or hearing impaired individuals.

Librarians can find employment with local government, college and university libraries, elementary and secondary school libraries, cities and county library systems, hospitals, and corporations as research consultants. Librarians can apply their information managements and research skills outside of the library as database development trainers and managers, and media specialists. Freelance librarians can become information brokers or document delivery specialists who provide services to other libraries, businesses, or government agencies.

The appropriate professional degree for a librarian is a master of library and information science (MLIS). Entry-level positions such as library clerks, assistants, and technicians typically do not require an MLIS degree. Indeed.com reports that the average salary for library scientists nationally is $57,000.[20]

Visit Library Careers (http://www.librarycareers.org) for more information about careers in library science.

CHAPTER TEN

Careers for Persuaders

20 years from now you will be more disappointed by the things you didn't do than by the ones you did do. So throw off the bowlines. Sail away from the safe harbor. Catch the trade winds in your sails. Explore. Dream. Discover.

—Mark Twain

How Do I Know If I'm a Persuader?

If you are a persuader, you will probably enjoy working in positions of leadership, power, and influence. Persuaders enjoy making decisions and leading others. They are not afraid of risk. Persuaders like to work with others to complete projects and achieve goals.

Persuaders are usually interested in careers in business, communications, management, sales, marketing, politics, law, or leadership.

Business Management

Business managers are found in all businesses, large and small. They make sure the company runs smoothly by overseeing the daily activities and managing its employees. In a large company, the manager's role is more focused on an individual department, such as marketing, sales, or production. In a smaller company, the business manager might be responsible for all departments in a company.

Managers must have interests and skills in people and data. They must have strong communication and leadership skills, be able to make sound business decisions, and have good problem-solving abilities. For a manager at any level, the bottom line is to make sure that the company reaches its performance and financial goals.

The starting salary for business administration/management majors with a bachelor's degree, according to NACE, was $48,936.[1] However, there is much room for growth—the BLS reported that the median annual wage for management occupations was $98,560 in May 2015, which was the highest wage of all the major occupational groups.[2]

For more information about careers in business, go to Careers in Business (http://careersinbusiness.com).

Communications

In an article by Dick Lee and Delmar Hatesohl posted on the University of Missouri Extension website, "A typical study points out that many of us spend 70 to 80 percent of our waking hours in some form of communication. Of that time, we spend about 9 percent writing, 16 percent reading, 30 percent speaking, and 45 percent listening."[3]

According to Communications-major.com, "A background in communications is highly regarded in business, marketing, education, politics, and public relations as if the ability to develop a targeted message and deliver it effectively is fundamental to success in these fields, and many others."[4]

Communications is a diverse and flexible field of study. At most colleges, communications is an umbrella degree that houses advertising, broadcasting, journalism, and public relations. If you're planning on being the next Diane Sawyer or Brian Williams, get a degree in broadcast journalism, mass communication, or journalism.

Advertising. Advertising serves as a communications mechanism for informing, persuading, and reminding consumers about products, services, and brands. Advertising uses graphic communications to visually represent and transmit messages to the public. Advertising graduates are creative individuals who work well with people. They are also skilled in using modern computer graphics software. There are several positions within the advertising industry: advertising salesperson, advertising manager, art director, and graphic designer. A college degree is preferred. Average starting salary: $37,830.

Radio, television, and digital broadcasting. The field of broadcasting is going through a period of rapid change. The advent of digital technologies and nonbroadcast video has changed the face of traditional broadcasting and now includes all forms of radio, television, and online media.

Most of the attention is usually given to the on-air "personalities" on radio and television, but the people behind the scenes (production staff, engineers, managers, and salespeople) make up the bulk of the industry's employment.

Broadcasting is a highly competitive field, and a college education is becoming key to standing out from the crowd. Experience is also critical, so graduates should try to gain experience in any avenue that they can, even small, part-time positions. It is common for professionals in this field to begin their careers at small or rural markets or independent production facilities and work their way up to networks and larger markets. A bachelor's degree is preferred, but associate degree graduates can find entry-level positions. Average annual starting salary: $31,090.

Journalism. Journalism is the art and science of researching and gathering information and communicating it to the public through writing, speaking, visual, or electronic means. Journalists inform the public about the latest news and events that are happening locally, nationally, and internationally. Journalists do not sit at a desk all day; they must go where the news is happening and then communicate that news via all forms of media outlets (i.e., newspapers, magazines, webcasts, radio, television) to reach their audience.

Currently, the industry standard is a bachelor's degree in journalism or communication, although associate degree journalism graduates can find entry-level journalism positions with newspapers and magazines. In college, journalism majors are typically required to choose an area of specialization. Average starting salary: $37,269.

Public relations. Communications-Major.com underscores the importance of the public relations field, "More than ever, thanks in part to the exponential growth of social media and communication technology, public relations managers and specialists have become the cornerstone liaisons between business organizations and the general public."[5] Companies and individuals hire public relations specialists to help them create and maintain a positive image in the media. Companies use public relations professions to create a positive public image, answer questions from consumers, and interact with the press.

Good writing and speaking skills are essential for success in this field as well as a background in media production. A bachelor's degree is preferred. Average starting salary: $37,830.

(*Note*: Salaries for advertising, broadcasting, journalism, and public relations were taken from National Association of Colleges and Employers, *Fall 2016 Salary Survey*.[6])

Table 10.1   Jobs in Communications

Advertising	
Advertising manager	Art/creative director
Copywriter	Editor
Marketing director	Marketing research manager
Product development	Promotions director
Public relations manager	Social media manager

Journalism	
Assistant editor	Copywriter
Editor	Junior copywriter
Journalist	News assignment desk
Photojournalist	

Sports/Entertainment	
Press agent	Press agent trainee
Sports team publicist	Theatrical press agent
Theatrical press agent apprentice	Unit publicist

Hospitality	
Director public information	Hotel/resort advertising assistant
Hotel/resort publicist	Nightclub/restaurant publicist
Restaurant/club advertising manager	

Non-Profit Agencies	
Advertising assistant	Director of public relations, hospital
Director of fund-raising	Community relations coordinator, police
Guest service coordinator	Volunteer coordinator

Corporate/Industry	
Advertising manager	Copywriter
Communications specialist	Consumer relations representative
Fund-raiser	Development officer
Employee relations coordinator	Media buyer
Publications researcher	Public information officer
Public relations manager	Recruiter
Sales manager	Social media manager

(*Continued*)

Corporate/Industry

Special events coordinator	Speech writer
Trade show representative	Volunteer coordinator

Radio/Television

Advertising copywriter	Advertising production assistant
Advertising sales assistant	Advertising sales representative
Community news/events director	Managing editor
News anchor	Producer
Production crew	Promotion coordinator
Public relations assistant	Radio announcer
Reporter	Sports director
Station manager	Traffic assistant
Traffic manager	

Miscellaneous

Director of public relations, college	Press secretary, government/political
Social media manager, college	Sports information director, college

Freelance

Freelance speechwriter	Freelance copywriter
Freelance acquisitions editor	Public relations generalist
VIP coordinator	

Law

One of the most frequently asked questions is: What are the best college majors and activities for law school preparation? The American Bar Association does not recommend any one undergraduate major to prepare for law school. They state, "Whatever major you select, you are encouraged to pursue an area of study that interests and challenges you, while taking advantage of opportunities to develop your research and writing skills."[7]

Many people assume a major in American history or political science, combined with public speaking or student government activities, is the best preparation for law school. But legal pretraining during college isn't necessary for admission into law school. In fact, students are admitted to law school from almost every academic major.

According to Shauna C. Bryce, Esquire, "What's far more critical is a student's pre-training in *thinking like a lawyer*."[8]

She says that the skills needed are the following:

- Critical thinking
- Creative thinking
- Evaluation of different perspectives
- Oral and written communication

So what types of activities build these skills? Most law school advisors recommend taking as many courses that will develop skills in research, critical thinking, writing, and public speaking as possible.

According to the Bureau of Labor Statistics, "Employment of lawyers is projected to grow 6 percent from 2014 to 2024, about as fast as the average for all occupations. Competition for jobs should continue to be strong because more students graduate from law school each year than there are jobs available."[9] The average annual salary for lawyers was $115,820 in 2015, but that varies widely by specialty and geographic area.[10]

Marketing

Marketing is a broad business concept that includes every aspect of creating and distributing products and services to people including developing a product, pricing, distribution, promotional strategy, and customer relationships.

Sales is a component of marketing, but marketing differs from sales because it is concerned with developing a demand for a product and fulfilling the customer's needs, not just getting customers to buy your product.

Professional marketers must be able to analyze international and national markets, understand and recognize consumer choices, possess creativity, and be able to work in a team environment. Most entry-level marketing positions will require a bachelor's degree in marketing, but upper-level management positions often require a master's degree. According to NACE, the average starting salary for a marketing graduate with a bachelor's degree was $44,841 and $55,993 for a master's degree.[11]

Political Science and Government

The field of political science can prepare you for a variety of fulfilling careers in public service from city major to state representative to the president of the United States. Because political science is a liberal arts degree, it will also provide the necessary core courses to qualify you for roles in the state or federal government, law school, or business.

The American Political Science Association suggests, "Minoring or double-majoring in a related social science or humanities discipline—such as history, philosophy, economics, or sociology—can complement the study of political science and broaden your career prospects."[12]

Visit the American Political Science Association (http://www.apsanet .org) for more information about careers in political science.

Table 10.2   Jobs in Politics and Government

Political Campaigns	
Campaign manager	Political consultant
Political party staffer	Pollster
Political Office	
City counselor	District attorney
Governor	Mayor
President of the United States	School board member
U.S. representative	U.S. senator
State Government	
Administrative assistant	Management analyst
Program manager	Public information officer
State representative	State senator
Local Government	
Assessor	Economic developer
Election official	Housing specialist
Local political aide	Mayor
Municipal clerk	Recreation supervisor
Town/city manager	Urban and regional planner
Zoning officer	
Local/State Specialists	
County engineer	Emergency manager
Employment interviewer/counselor	Environmental specialist
Labor relations specialist	Public health professional
Victim advocate	

(Continued)

Table 10.2 (Continued)

Community, Social, and International Issues	
Community development associate	Community organizer
Conflict resolution specialist	Human rights advocate
Peace worker	Women's rights activist

Lobbies, Unions, and Associations	
Labor union organizer	Lobbyist
Membership director, association	Political action committee (PAC)

Service Programs	
AmeriCorps member	Antidiscrimination worker
Auditor	Ethics investigator
Human services director	Peace corps volunteer

State/Federal Legislative Staff	
Chief of staff	Congressional page
District aide	Legislative assistant
Legislative correspondent	Research analyst

Other State/Federal Positions	
Government lawyer	Paralegal
Policy analyst	Press secretary
Speechwriter	

International Affairs	
Foreign service officer	Intelligence operative
United Nations headquarters intern	

Nonprofit Advocacy and Administration	
Communication director	Director of volunteers
Executive director	Founder, nonprofit organization
Fund-raiser	Program assistant
Program director	Program officer, foundation

Public Interest	
Consumer activist	Environmental activist
Government reform activist	Lobbyist

Politicians who hold executive positions such as mayor, county commissioner, or city manager have wide variations in their salaries depending upon their jurisdiction. According to Payscale.com, the salary for a city mayor in the United States averaged about $62,000 per year.[13] Salaries among state legislators also vary widely. At the high end, California's legislators earn $100,113/year, $14,774 more per year than the next highest-paid lawmakers in Pennsylvania ($85,339/year).[14] At the lower end, legislators in Texas earn the lowest yearly salary, at $7,200 per year, and legislators in New Mexico make no salary, although they do earn $163/day in per diem.[15]

Sales

Sales careers are everywhere—if a company makes a product or provides a service, the only way it can make any money is to sell that product or service to someone else. Home appliances, computer stores, and clothing stores have in-store salespeople. Outside sales positions involve selling goods and supplies to businesses (e.g., copy machines to a school or business, radio advertising space to a nonprofit organization, dental supplies to a dentist, and pharmaceutical drugs to doctors and veterinarians). Even the admissions staff in your college or university could be considered salespeople—especially if they tried to convince you to attend their college.

People in sales usually have interests and skills in people and often are persuasive in nature. They value success, status, and initiative and are often described as ambitious, outgoing, and enthusiastic. To effectively serve their customers, they must have excellent communication and people skills. Sales is among the few careers where you can make as much money as you want to, based on your level of effort and skill. The average starting salary, according to the NACE, was $50,122.[16]

CHAPTER ELEVEN

Gathering Data for Good Decision-Making

The doors we open and close each day decide the lives we live.
—Flora Whittemore

There are literally thousands of career opportunities available in the working world. The *Dictionary of Occupational Titles* lists over 12,000 different occupations and colleges, and universities offer anywhere from 50 to 200 different majors depending on the size of the institution. But how do you know which career to choose? And what college major will best prepare you for success in that career? Just reading the college catalog isn't enough, although it is a good place to start. What are the requirements of all of these different programs of study? How do they relate to your own aptitudes and interests? What jobs will those majors lead to?

There are upsides and downsides to every career. The trick is to find the one that fits you the best—your strengths, your personality, your work habits. And the only way to determine that is to do some serious research. Go on the Internet, ask your teachers, and talk to neighbors or family members. If you're interested in becoming a physical therapist, call a local rehab center and see if there is someone who would spend a few minutes talking to you about his or her career. Before you can make a realistic decision about your major, it's important to take an informed look at all the possibilities.

Many students choose a career based on what their friends are doing or what is popular in the media rather on what will be best for *them* in the future. That's why it's important to get the facts. Many students think they want to pursue forensic science after watching CSI only to find out that those positions require a science background or even medical training. Without thoroughly researching their intended careers, many students happily complete a major in college only to go into the work world and find out their job was not all they expected it to be.

Making an "informed" career decision means making a career decision based on *all* available information. That means looking beyond the surface of a possible career and determining such things as which occupations have a decent starting salary, are projected to do well in the future, have openings in your geographic area, and won't be outsourced any time soon.

Based on the information you gathered in the previous chapters, you should be able to identify the following features about yourself:

1.   Interests
2.   Hobbies
3.   Strengths
4.   Personality style
5.   Work values

If you need more help identifying your interests, strengths, values, and personality style, review Chapter 4 or make an appointment with a career counselor/coach in your college career center.

Connecting People to Occupations

A good career match is made when the essential factors that make up an individual (interests, values, ability, and personality style) align with the essential attributes of a job or career. In a more practical example, think of all the skills that are involved in being a receptionist in a medical office. In order to be a successful, you would want a person who (a) likes people (interests); (b) takes pleasure from being helpful and being part of a larger team (values); (c) is energized by a fast-paced, often noisy or crowded, and sometimes unpredictable working environment (personality style); and (d) has good verbal communication skills, organizational ability, and computer or office technology skills (aptitude). Good receptionists are not only people oriented but possess good clerical, computer, and organizational skills as well. The point is that you have to look at *all* of the factors that make up a job and see how well they fit with *all* of the factors that make up a person, not just one. Just because someone enjoys "being with people" doesn't necessarily mean they'd make a good medical receptionist. If that particular individual also happens to be extremely verbal and creative and prefers to deal with situations as they arise, rather than following an established routine, then that medical office is probably going to end up in chaos. This particular individual might be better suited in a public relations, marketing, or fund-raising career where there is more personal flexibility and the opportunity to exercise creativity and spontaneity.

If you still need help identifying your strengths, interests, values, and personality style, make an appointment with a career counselor in your college career center.

After reading Chapters 5–10, you should now be able to identify if you are primarily a "compassionate," "creative," "hands-on," "analytical," "organizer," or "persuader" type of individual. You may even have been able to choose a couple of job titles from one of those categories. Now you're ready to begin narrowing your choices by researching individual majors or occupations within the one or two broad career areas that you have chosen.

How to Research Careers

Sometimes students select, or are advised to select, majors based on a small piece of information. Think about how many people pick engineering simply because they're "good at math." The field of engineering is much more than *just math*. And while engineering may be an appropriate option for someone who has an affinity for math, there are hundreds of other math-related careers and jobs that may be just as rewarding. That's why doing your occupational research is so important.

Here's how you should gather information on the career fields that you are considering:

- Research potential careers and learn about job descriptions, educational requirements, and the skills necessary for success.
- Learn more about a career by conducting an informational interview with a professional in your chosen field.
- Shadow a professional at work to see what he or she does on a daily basis.
- Test the waters further by finding career-related summer and part-time jobs.
- Get some in-depth experience by obtaining an internship or service-learning position.
- Make sure there's an active job market for the major that you choose.

The O*NET Resource Center is a good place to begin researching careers. It can be accessed online at http://online.onetcenter.org and contains detailed descriptions of hundreds of occupations. Or, if you prefer, another very easy way to find information about careers is to use your Internet browser (Google, Yahoo, etc.). Simply type "Careers in (accounting, automotive, animals, fashion design, etc.)" in the search box to access a wealth of career-related websites about a career of interest.

How to Do Internet Research

Where do I start? Which sites should I choose? How do I know this site will give me accurate information? Before you begin, there are some things you need to remember when using the Internet. One is that the Internet is constantly changing. Sites often move to new addresses. If you type in an address, or URL (uniform resource locator), for a site that has moved to a different location, you will usually receive a prompt telling you to wait a few seconds while you are automatically forwarded to the new location. Remember to make a note of the new URL, or add it to your bookmarks.

You may get a message that the page you are looking for doesn't exist or can no longer be found. In that case, try searching for the site by using one of the many search engines available today. Although the specific page you are looking for may have changed, the home page may still be active. This is quite common in college and university sites. In this case, log into the college's home page (e.g., http://www.college.edu) and then try searching for whatever specific page you are looking for. It is for this reason that many of the websites listed in this book have short URL addresses, followed by instructions on how to proceed to a specific page (rather than providing the entire URL address).

When doing an Internet search, you can narrow the search results by placing quotation marks around the word, phrase, or title of whatever you are looking for (e.g., "Science Careers"). The search engine will search only for sites containing that specific phrase. If you just simply type in "Science Careers," without quotation marks, then the database will search for *any* website containing those words or phrase that can result in hundreds of websites.

Another key factor to remember is to type in the web address *exactly* as it appears. Even one incorrect keystroke can take you to a totally unrelated site. Most websites will have addresses ending in *.edu*, *.org*, *.com*, or *.gov*. These extensions, or "domains," can help you identify the content in a website. Domain names ending in *.edu* are usually assigned to educational organizations (colleges and universities), *.org* to nonprofit organizations, *.com* to commercial or personal websites, and. *gov* to government sites. By noting the domain you can determine, in advance, if a site is going to be reputable. I generally begin my search by looking at sites from educational, government, or professional organizations (*.edu*, *.gov*, or *.org*). Commercial (*.com*) sites may or may not be reputable. As the number of websites on the Internet increases, you may see some exceptions. For example, an organization may have to use. com or. net instead of. org if the name they wanted is already registered with someone else. So when you find a good site with factual information from professional in that field, bookmark it or write down the URL.

General career exploration websites are a good starting place for gathering general career information and exploring options. Some of these sites offer a variety of career-related information such as self-assessments, information about the career planning process, steps to follow in your decision-making journey, and information about majors. Some examples of general career exploration sites are College Career Life Planning (http://www.collegecareerlifeplanning.com) and My Next Move (http://www.mynextmove.org).

Websites for high school students are directly targeted to the interests and concerns of high school students. Some of these sites contain assessments, career profiles, or magazine articles. One example is Jobs Made Real (http://www.jobsmadereal.com). This site is made for teens and by teens and has a collection of videos that tells you what a job is really like.

College and university websites, while certainly not limited to college-aged students, are primarily websites of academic departments at colleges and universities. These sites offer a wealth of in-depth information about specific college majors and the careers they can lead to, related career titles, and job projections. High school juniors and seniors will also find these sites invaluable not only to research individual majors but to research potential colleges that offer the majors they are interested in. As new jobs and new job titles emerge in the workforce, colleges generally respond by adding and modifying the majors they offer. So by surfing some of these college websites, you may discover a new or related major you never knew existed.

When you have learned as much as possible through print resources or the Internet, it's time to talk to people who do the kind of work that interests you.

Informational Interviewing

Informational interviewing, or asking other people about their jobs, is a great way to get some insider information about a particular career. Here are examples of the types of questions to ask:

- Why did you choose this career?
- What was your major in college?
- What are the educational requirements for this job or profession?
- Are there any additional licenses or certifications that are necessary?
- What are your main responsibilities or job duties?
- What do you like and what do you dislike about this occupation?
- Describe a typical day on your job.
- What types of people, clients, patients, customers, and so on do you interact with on a daily basis?
- What is the average starting salary for this job?
- What does it take to be successful in this career?
- Do you have any advice for someone considering this career?

Start by asking your professors and family members if they know of anyone who would be willing to sit down with you for 30 minutes and talk about their career. Ask your career center or your academic advisor to assist you if necessary.

Job Shadowing

Job shadowing is another way to obtain information about a career—actually, it's the next best thing to actually being on the job. Shadowing is simply following a professional around for a morning or afternoon and watching what they do during their job. Not only can you observe first-hand what that individual does and who they interact with on a daily basis, but you can ask questions to decide if this is a job that you want to do.

Rebecca

Rebecca was a second-year student who came to see me for career counseling. She had done her career research and thought that she might be interested in physical therapy but wasn't sure. I suggested that she make arrangements to shadow a physical therapist at our local rehabilitation center. After completing the job shadow, she e-mailed me and said,

"I'm going to cancel our appointment today because I shadowed a physical therapist yesterday and it was a wonderful experience! Now I'm absolutely sure that that (physical therapy) is what I would like to do for my career."

How cool is that?

Use your school's career center to help you arrange a shadowing opportunity. Begin contacting companies that have formed partnerships with your school. If that doesn't work, ask your professors for possible contacts.

Professional Organizations

Professional organization websites are a great source of information about careers. Most careers are affiliated with a professional organization or accrediting body that maintains the educational and professional standards for the profession. Each professional organization has a website dedicated to providing support and resources to its members and advancing the profession by providing career information and the latest news, research, or advocacy activity. Most of these websites have a Career tab that clearly explains what the profession does, the educational requirements, and the career opportunities in that field. A list of professional organizations can be found in Appendix B.

In addition to having an informative website, most national organizations also have state, local, and student chapters on college campuses. Check to see if your campus has a student organization—it's a great way to learn about the profession and connect with professionals in your area.

Employment Trends

Every two years, the U.S. Bureau of Labor Statistics revises its 10-year projections of industry and occupational employment. The most current employment projections can be found on the Bureau of Labor Statistics website at http://www.bls.gov. For a detailed summary of these projections, check out the *Occupational Outlook Handbook* (OOH) at http://www.bls.gov/ooh. The OOH is one of the nation's most widely used sources of career information and covers about 80 percent of occupations.

So where will the jobs be in the next 10 years? Pretty much where they've been in the past several years—in the health-care and service industries. As the baby boom population ages, the demand for all health-care services will continue to increase.

According to the Bureau of Labor Statistics, the top-20 fastest-growing occupations for 2014 to 2024 include: wind turbine service techs, occupational and physical therapy assistants, physical therapy and home health aides, commercial divers, nurse practitioners, physical therapists, statisticians, ambulance drivers, occupational therapy aides, physician assistants, operation research analysts, personal financial advisors, cartographers/photogrammetrists, genetic counselors, interpreters/translators, audiologists and hearing aide specialists, and optometrists.[1]

The majority of the fastest-growing occupations enjoy a high salary but also require a bachelor's degree or higher. Keep in mind that fast growth (highest percent change of employment) does not necessarily equate to a large number of job openings.

Employment trends are influenced by economic factors, population demographics, social trends, and public policies. The growing number of baby boomers entering retirement age not only affects the number of jobs available for younger workers but has largely fueled the strong demand for nursing, occupational, physical therapy, and home health-care occupations. For those of you have taken an economics course, the basic principles of supply and demand largely govern the job market. The rise and fall of the dot-com industry is a perfect example. Emerging in the late 1990s, hundreds of Internet industries sprang up, offering the promise of getting rich fast. Along with that was an abundance of IT jobs with those start-up companies. Students didn't even have to have a degree to get a good-paying job—just good programming skills or a catchy new idea. I was working at a four-year college at the time and distinctly remember a student telling me that he had decided to drop out of school because he got a really good-paying job with a new dot-com company. The stock market crash around the year 2000 ended the dot-com bubble and ended employment for many IT workers, including, I'm sure, that student. Jobs in the IT field were hard to come by even for students who did complete their degrees.

Consider Your Desired Lifestyle

Too often do students choose a major without really considering how it will fit with their life plans. The career you choose should fit into *your* lifestyle, not the other way around. For example, if you want financial security and time to raise a family, becoming an over-the-road truck driver or high-powered marketing or television correspondent may not be the job for you. However, a good teaching position that has a year-round salary plan and evenings and summers off may provide you with the steady income and time off to raise a family.

Based on your desired lifestyle, what would your perfect job look like? Be as specific as possible, describe it in detail, and right down to the type of office decor you would choose.

As you begin researching careers, make a list of the ones that you are interested in and that seem to best fit your values, personality style, and skills and abilities. Once you've selected several options, go back and research their educational requirements. What major (or majors) do you need to take in college? What type of degree is required? Will additional schooling or training beyond a bachelor's degree be required? If you're in middle school or high school, find out what courses you will need to take in high school to prepare you for the postsecondary training you'll need to complete after high school. In other words, look into the future and identify your career goal. Then work your way back through college or high school to whatever educational level you are now and map out what courses you'll need to take to eventually reach that goal. And remember, in some cases, *several* majors or degrees may lead to the same destination.

Questions to Ask Yourself

Spend some time thinking about the questions and answer them as honestly and as completely as you can. Remember, short of actually doing the job, your ability to make a solid career decision will only be as good as the information you gather.

Use the following questions as a guide when researching an occupation or career:

1. **Description**. What exactly does a person in this career do on a daily basis? Does this career require you to work primarily with people, data, ideas, or machines? (Will you enjoy these duties?)

2. **Work hours**. Are the work hours during the daytime, evening, swing shift, 40 hours a week, or longer? Will you be expected to work overtime? (Will this work schedule fit into your lifestyle?)

3. **Work environment**. Will you be working in an office environment, on the road, in a plant, in a hospital or clinic, or outdoors? Will you be part of a team or expected to work independently? How much autonomy or decision-making ability will you have? Is this a faster-paced or slower-paced work environment? What is the stress level in this job? (Does this work environment complement your personality style?)

4. **Salary and benefits**. What is the starting wage or salary? Is the pay based on an hourly rate, annual salary, or commission? Are you paid weekly,

monthly, or bimonthly? Are there opportunities for bonuses, raises, or advancement? What do you need to do to be successful in this career? (Is the salary and benefits enough to live on? Will they allow you to have the type of lifestyle that you want?)

5. **Credentials**. What are the minimal requirements to enter this profession? What educational degree, training, certification, licensing, or skills are required to enter this profession? Are there any special personal attributes, mental capacities, or physical requirements needed to perform the job tasks in this career? (Do you have the ability, resources, and motivation to complete these requirements?)

6. **Occupational outlook**. What is the future job outlook for this career? Will there be a demand for this occupation 5 or 10 years from now, or is the industry subject to economic fluctuations or local labor market demand?

7. What are the advantages and disadvantages of working in this career?

8. How well does this career match your interests, strengths, values, motivation, and personality style?

9. Will this career allow you to achieve what you want out of life?

After doing your research, you should now be ready to narrow your choices to one or two college majors (e.g., business or engineering). If you're still relatively undecided in your choice of major or career, try to select a career "cluster" like "health care" or "science." Then research the occupations within that cluster and narrow down your selections. Don't worry about choosing a specialty area or option within a major at this time. You'll be ready to do that after you've been exposed to more courses in your major.

CHAPTER TWELVE

Connecting College Majors to Careers

Our society needs both plumbers and philosophers, or neither our theories nor our pipes will hold water.

—John Gardner

In today's turbulent economic times, everyone who attends college is keenly focused on being able to make the best use of his or her investment by successfully securing employment at graduation. Everyone has heard stories of college students who were not able to find a job in his or her major, thus adding to the general level of pressure heaped on college students to pick the "right" major.

However, students in any major can greatly improve their chances of finding employment by knowing how to look for openings and how to market themselves accordingly.

Many students think major = career. "Major" is an academic term, part of the process of earning an education. "Career" is the actual job or profession that one does over their lifetime.

Some majors have a *direct* relationship to careers:

Major	Occupation
Accounting	accountant
Nursing	nurse
Education	teacher

Most majors have only an *indirect* relationship with careers and, as a result, may lead to several jobs or more than one career:

Major	*Occupations*
English	editor, public relations, teacher, lawyer
Communications	broadcasting, public relations, advertising, sales, college admissions

All majors will lead to a job after graduation—some are less visible than others, which may mean that you will have to search harder and be more creative to find them. What matters most is that you have the proper combination of *education*, *skills*, and *experience* needed for a particular job.

When trying to find a major, it will be helpful for high school and college students to think about your goal first:

Career = Future Big Picture Goal

Then backtrack from your big picture goal and determine what degree(s), skills, and other requirements you will need to reach that career goal.

Career → Work Experience → Licensure, Certifications, and so on.
→ Graduate or Undergraduate College Degree → Major

Baccalaureate versus Associate Degrees

A baccalaureate (four-year) degree in business, for example, is not just made up of one job, but it is comprised of many different specialty areas including accounting, actuarial science, economics, finance, information systems, international business, logistics, management, human resources, sales, real estate, and marketing. All these areas, or *majors*, relate to specific job functions in the business world. Majoring in one area allows you to do study those specific areas in depth over a period of four years.

Associate (two-year) degrees are generally more career-oriented. They contain fewer core courses because they are designed to place graduates directly into the workforce after two years of study. There is usually a very clear path between major and job. Examples are plumbing and heating, electrical, registered nursing, culinary, veterinary technician, and computer information systems. Now to make things even more confusing, some majors, like business and computer information systems, have two- and four-year degree options. Two-year degree options offer a sampling of specialty areas (breadth) but not the depth of their four-year counterparts.

Certificate programs are short term, intense training programs that are designed to provide job seekers with a set of skills (e.g., dental assisting, medical coding, phlebotomy, EKG, nurses aid, welding, and plumbing). The advantage is short term and can get you into the job market quickly. In many circumstances, students can continue their education after earning a certificate by "stepping up" to an associate degree.

Translating Majors into Jobs

One of the problems that students have is being able to connect their major to job opportunities in the marketplace. The task is easier for students who major in professional degrees like education and accounting, but more difficult for students in the liberal arts. Add to that confusion is the reality that some jobs require a particular major and others prefer a set of skills and some related work experience. Even professional majors can lead to jobs outside the realm of a traditional position. This is good news, because in a tight economy where teaching jobs, for example, may be scarce, opportunities could exist in educational sales, customer service, corporate training, or entry-level positions in business. It's all about knowing what skills employers want and thinking outside of the employment box.

Payscale.com has a fun tool called GigZig (https://www.payscale.com/gigzig.aspx) that shows the career paths of real people. Simply type in a job title or career and wait for the results to display. In the middle column, you'll see a list of related careers. In the left column, there is a list of jobs that people had before they moved into the position that you selected. In the right column, you will see future jobs—the jobs that people moved into after your job.

Let's begin by looking at the differences between the college system and the job market. In general, college majors are usually housed under a broad academic disciplines like communications, health care, education, or business. The job market, on the other hand, is organized by industry and job function. Some examples of industry sectors are education, sales, and publishing. Examples of job functions within these industries would be an elementary teacher, inside sales representative, and editor. If you read the description of any job opening, you'll find that each position requires a requisite amount of training/education, certification, or licensing; a list of skills; or a specified number of years of experience. In the work world, skills, experience, and education matter most to employers.

The trick is being able to extract the knowledge, skills, and experiences obtained in your major and translate them into the language of the workforce (i.e., skills, degrees, experience).

Most employers are looking for employees who have the ability to problem-solve, work in teams, write and communicate, and think critically. Graduates who can clearly articulate the value they can bring to an employer by illustrating their technical and soft skills, related work experience, and unique knowledge in their major will be the most successful in the job market after graduation.

Professional versus Liberal Arts Degrees

Professional careers are those that lead directly to a career. Education majors will be educators, engineering majors will become engineers, and accounting majors will become accountants. These majors are providing professional preparation for a specific job or set of jobs based on standards or requirements dictated by the individual profession. Education majors take a strict sequence of classes to prepare them to become teachers and must take and pass a licensure exam after graduation before they can receive a teacher's license in their particular state. Likewise, engineering students must take and pass the PE (professional engineer) exam to practice.

Other college majors, like those in the liberal arts (majors like history, sociology, religious studies, communications, and philosophy) are designed to prepare students for not one, but a *variety* of jobs, in the workforce. Liberal arts students possess written and oral communication skills, critical thinking, the ability to conduct research, and an appreciation for other cultures. Language skills and multicultural sensitivity are highly marketable skills in today's workplace. The skills acquired in a liberal arts education can be used in the business world, at a nonprofit agency, in government, as a customer service supervisor, in sales, or in the admissions or registrar's office of a college or university. As Katherine Brooks, EdD, author of *You Majored in What?: Mapping Your Path from Chaos to Career*, said in an interview, "Liberal arts students have "potential"—that's what they're selling to an employer."[1]

If you have a variety of interests, you might be interested in creating an interdisciplinary major. An interdisciplinary major allows you to combine several subjects around a unified theme on a topic that is not usually offered as a major. Student who are interested in pursuing this option should work closely with their academic advisor or department chair as early as possible.

What Can I Do with a Liberal Arts Degree?

Liberal arts degrees often get a bum rap. But liberal arts students have the skills that employers are looking for in today's candidates. The *Job Outlook 2016* survey by the NACE showed that the top-five skills that employers want to see in candidates are leadership, ability to work in a team, written communication, problem-solving, and verbal communication.[2] These skills can be acquired from class, on an internship, in a clinical or research setting, through a service-learning project, on a part-time job, or through extracurricular activities on your campus. The key is to understand how to apply a set of skills from a philosophy or history degree, for example, to the job market. Job descriptions list the skills they are looking for in a position under the job requirements. If a job requires some research ability, did you do a research project in one of your courses? If an employer is looking for someone with problem-solving ability, can you pull out some examples of a problem-solving approach that you learned in class? Know what skills employers are looking for and emphasize those on your resume.

The Hanover College Career Center, located in Hanover, Indiana, created a handy handout called, "Liberal Arts Skills at Work." It lists the ways in which you can develop these skills in your classes and how employers utilize them in the workplace.

Table 12.1   Liberal Arts Skills at Work

Writing Skills

Developed in class:
- Term papers
- Essay tests
- Lab reports
- Notebooks
- Article summaries
- Journals
- Creative writing
- Case reports
- Internship essays
- Peer reviews
- Literature reviews

Table 12.2   Speaking Skills

Developed in class:

- In-class presentations, reports
- Classes that base grades on, or that encourage, participation in class discussions
- Speeches
- Theater performances
- Group projects
- Study groups
- Convocations
- Good papers project
- Internship presentations

Table 12.3   Research and Analysis

Developed in class:

- Research papers
- Field studies
- Independent study
- Independent grant research
- Independent laboratory research
- Internship essays
- Literature reviews
- Case studies
- Journal article critiques
- Analysis and critique of arguments during class and in papers

Source: Reproduced with permission of Margaret Krantz, Hanover College, the copyright holder.

History

History is an example of a liberal arts career. Although history-related positions can be found with museums and historical sites, there are also opportunities as a research librarian, documentary writer, historical researcher, secondary and postsecondary teacher, historical advocate or lobbyist, grant writer, college admissions staff, and nonprofit administrator. For more information about careers for history majors, visit the American Historical Association at http://www.historians.org/pubs/free/careers /Index.htm.

Table 12.4   Jobs for History Majors

Education

Secondary history teacher	College professor
College student affairs staff	College admissions staff
Alumni affairs staff	Development staff
Historic site education specialist	Museum guide and education specialist

Communications

Author, writer	Documentary writer/editor
Editor, magazine, book, publication	Journalist
Public relations	Speechwriter

Information Management

Archivist	Records manager/staff
Research librarian	

Research

Genealogist	Historical researcher
Museum historian	

Legal

Historical advocate paralegal	Lawyer
Legislative staff	Litigation support

Business

Consultant	Grant writer
Foundation board staff	Nonprofit director/administrator
Researcher	

Jobs That Require No Particular Major

There are jobs that rely more on a skill set or employee attitude than their type of degree. Employers usually want employees who have some type of education (this shows that they're trainable or educated), but they don't require a particular major. The field of business is a great example: with an unrelated degree, but plenty of relevant work experience, a person can be very successful in the business world.

Students who major in English, business, computer information systems, history, foreign language, criminal justice, prelaw, political science, mathematics, and social sciences can emphasize a particular set of skills and college experiences to qualify for any of the above positions in the workforce. Students can even add another major or a minor to make themselves more marketable when applying for that first job. Adding a Spanish minor, for example, can make any major more marketable in today's world.

Table 12.5   Examples of Careers That Do Not Require Any Particular Major

Account executive	Credit manager	Manufacturer's sales representative
Administrative assistant	Curator	
Advertising worker	Customer service rep.	Marketing research worker
Air traffic controller	Customs inspector	
Announcer	Detective	Minister
Appraiser	Displayer, merchandise	Paralegal assistant
Athlete, professional	Editorial assistant	Peace Corp volunteer
Bailiff	Elected official	Police officer
Benefits manager	Employment interviewer	Priest
Broker's floor representative	Employment, rehabilitation	Private investigator
		Public relations worker
Buyer	Executive secretary	Publishing agent
Camp director	Financial planner	Quality assurance analyst
Childcare provider	Firefighter	
City manager	Flight attendant	Retail store manager
Claims adjuster	Food and drug inspector	Sales manager
Claims examiner	Foreign service officer	Sales representative
College student personnel worker	Fund-raiser/development officer	Special agent: FBI/ CIA, Secret Service/ Border Patrol
	Guide	
College administrator	Insurance agent/broker	Teacher aide
Columnist/commentator	Insurance examiner	Title examiner
Community organization worker	Labor relations worker	Transportation agent
	Legislative advocate	Travel agent
Consultant	Loan interviewer	Underwriter
Contract administrator	Loan officer	Vista volunteer
Corrections officer	Management trainee	Writer

Entrepreneurship is a unique opportunity that may or may not require a particular degree (or any degree at all). A successful entrepreneur simply needs to have a really good idea and a way to create and sell his or her product or service. Granted some college majors, like business, lend themselves better than others to helping beginning entrepreneurs understand what's involved in running a business, but anyone can be an entrepreneur regardless of his or her major. Entrepreneurs in nonbusiness majors can always pick up a minor in business or take some relevant small business courses. The small business administration at http://www.sba.gov has a variety of resources including local small business development centers that provide guidance and assistance to small business owners, especially women, with writing business plans and securing loans.

Should You Go to Graduate School?

Graduate education requires a significant financial and personal investment. You want to be able to dedicate as much of your time and energy as possible toward earning your degree and enjoying and making the most of your grad school experience. There are a number of advantages of going to graduate school. In general, the starting salary for a master's or doctoral degree holder is usually higher than an undergraduate degree. Continuing on to graduate school also temporarily delays repaying student loans. If you are interested in teaching or doing research at the college level, getting a PhD can lead to a tenured faculty or research position at a university or college complete with research opportunities, facilities, and graduate teaching assistants. If you're concerned about the cost of attending graduate school, consider applying for scholarships and fellowship funding. Graduate programs in the sciences and engineering often over teaching or research assistantships that will cover the cost of tuition and give you a stipend for living expenses. Many graduate programs now offer online, part-time, evening, and weekend options in response to the growing number of older students returning to school. Take the time to research your options and choose what works best for your situation.

Several professional fields such as counseling, social work, library science, physical therapy, occupational therapy, and speech pathology require a master's degree to practice professionally. Students typically earn a related bachelor's degree, depending on their intended profession, and then continue on to graduate school to earn a master's degree before they can practice in their field. Other professions such as physicians, chiropractors, veterinarians, lawyers, optometrist, pharmacists, and dentists must attend three to four years of study in a professional program beyond the bachelor's degree and then must pass a state licensing exam to practice in their respective professions.

The new skills and knowledge you gain from your graduate education can position you for more opportunities for advancement in your career. Whatever your motivation for pursuing graduate school, make sure you understand what a graduate program involves—financially, mentally, and emotionally.

CHAPTER THIRTEEN

Making Big Career Decisions

Everything in your life is a reflection of a choice you have made. If you want a different result, make a different choice.

—Unknown

Although we've discussed how to make a good career decision, I want to emphasize that what you are choosing today is a *soft* career decision. We can make as many plans as we want to, but the reality is that our plans may change. We may run into some kind of unexpected difficulty that causes us to alter our career plans. Once we get into the workforce we may decide to pursue another direction. A life event such as marriage, divorce, illness, or corporate downsizing may occur, and we adjust accordingly. As we grow and develop and acquire more skills and experiences, we will experience things and end up in places and situations that we would never have been able to predict when we were younger. And that's probably a good thing.

Are You Ready to Make a Career Decision?

The first step in making a career decision is to determine what decision or decisions need to be made. Some students are totally clueless about what they want to do with their lives, while others have their choices narrowed down to one or two majors. Are you ready to make a career decision? How do you feel about your ability to make a good decision?

To determine if you're ready to make a career decision, ask yourself these questions:

- Do I know my interests, abilities, values, and work style?
- Am I aware of the career options that are out there in the workforce?

- Have I narrowed my choices down to one or two careers?
- Have I thoroughly researched those options? When you are investigating a career, if something about that career doesn't feel right, then try to understand why. Is one aspect of the career overshadowing the others? Are there other important factors that have not been considered?
- Do I feel confident that I can make a good career decision based on my present circumstances and future goals?

If you've answered "yes" to all of these questions, you are ready to make a decision. If not, then reread previous chapters or continue to work with your career center until you feel ready to make a decision.

How We Make Decisions

All of us make hundreds of decision each day, from choosing what to wear in the morning to choosing what to eat for lunch. In fact, everything we say and do is the result of a decision, whether we make it consciously or not. How do you go about making decisions? Do you procrastinate? Seek the advice of others? Jump on the first choice that seems reasonable?

When it comes to making a career choice, most people don't use any process at all. They listen to everyone else—friends, parents (not that you shouldn't consider their advice), and even popular media instead of making their own career decision. Because there is no crystal ball to predict how our lives will turn out, the only thing we can do is to make the best decision we can with the information we have at the time, and try to prepare for any contingencies. Making a decision doesn't mean you can't change your mind down the road. You will have many opportunities to make adjustments in the future.

There are four main decision-making styles: (1) *rational*, (2) *intuitive*, (3) *dependent*, and (4) *avoidant*.

Rational decisions are made in a logical fashion and are based on facts. Intuitive decisions are based on feelings and emotional responses. Dependent decisions are based on what others think and feel, and avoidant decision-makers, also called "procrastinators," want to delay making a decision as long as possible. Read the following descriptions of each type of decision-making and see which method you prefer.

Rational

The rational or systematic decision-making method is when individuals use analysis, facts, and a step-by-step process to come to a decision.

They collect information and then weigh the pros and cons (i.e., advantages and disadvantages) of that information before making a decision.

Decision-Making Confidence.com outlines the five steps in a rational decision-making model:

- Research and identify options
- Compare and contrast each alternative and its consequences
- Make a decision or choose an alternative
- Design and implement an action plan
- Evaluate results[1]

Many people use a spreadsheet filled with pros, cons, qualities, and rankings to help them make a decision. An easier method is to take a piece of paper and make two parallel columns, labeled pros and cons. Then list every pro and con that you can think of, based on your research about that career. Now give each item an "importance" value from 1 to 5. Add up the numbers in each column. You now have a numerical "answer." The disadvantage of using a pros and cons list is that you may not consider all of the options that can easily lead you to rationalize what you already believe.

Intuitive

Some people are very tuned into their feelings or instincts and use them as guides to decision-making. If you prefer to make a decision based on what *feels* right, rather on analyzing the facts, you are using an intuitive approach.

Psychologist Dr. Gary Klein suggests that people use an intuitive approach 90 percent of the time. He developed the recognition primed decision-making model, which says that in any situation there are cues or hints that allow people to recognize patterns. "Based on the pattern, the person chooses a particular course of action. They mentally rehearse it and if they think it will work, they do it. If they don't think it will work, they choose another and mentally rehearse that. As soon as they find one that they think will work, they do it."[2]

In intuitive decision-making, *how you feel* is a determining factor in making a decision. Some intuitive decision-makers take their time to make a decision or sleep on it overnight. Another strategy is to discuss the issue with someone else—friends, family members, or anyone who has made a similar decision. Talking about it can help you see your position more clearly.

Another technique is to use a visualization exercise. Here's an example:

> Find a quiet, calming place to close your eyes and relax as you imagine that you are in a particular career. Visualize what you are wearing; imagine how it feels to be dressed in these clothes. Where are you—in an office, in a hospital, on a manufacturing floor? What are you doing? Who are you working with? What equipment, tools, or technology are you working with? How do you feel about the work you are doing? Are you excited, interested, or bored?

Afterward, think very carefully about the picture you have created. Is it based on facts or preconceptions? What feelings, thoughts, or experiences did you have? What do these feelings or thoughts tell you about your choice of career? If you felt negative about the experience, try to pinpoint the source of the negativity. Have you or your goals changed as a result of this experience?

Dependent

Dependent decision-makers rely heavily on the opinions of others. They have a difficult time separating what they want from what others want of them. Dependent decision-makers often ask, "What do *you* think I should do?," or "What would *you* do if you were me?" Many students fall into this category because of the overwhelming pressure of trying to pick that one perfect career or major out of hundreds of prospects.

Avoidant

Avoidant decision-makers have a hard time making up their mind, not only about a career but about everything in their lives. The pressure of making a difficult decision creates a type of mental paralysis that leads to indecision. Instead of dealing with their indecision head on, they put it off. The avoidant decision-maker says things like, "I'll deal with it later," or "I just can't decide." Many students procrastinate making a decision about a major or career direction because of the amount of time it takes to explore all the options.

We all make decisions in different ways. The key is to make a balanced decision, using your head, your heart, and the advice of others. If you tend to be impulsive, try to back up your decision with some data. If you're inclined to be too analytical, try to involve more of your emotions or intuition. Take the time to make sure that you're comfortable with your decision, and that you've made the right choice, both on a rational and an emotional level.

Obstacles to Career Decision-Making

There are a variety of reasons why someone may struggle making career decisions or decisions in general. Here are some common reasons:

- Not enough information, including where to find information about careers and how to evaluate that information once it's obtained.

- Inadequate or inaccurate information. Basing your decision on hearsay, or using information that is out of date, biased, or just plain wrong.

- Too much information. Being overwhelmed by the sheer number of career choices and majors available or being unable to shift through the mounds of information available on the web. Too many choices can cause some people to become paralyzed in their decision-making.

- Limited experience in making decisions.

- Lack of confidence in your ability to make a decision.

- Competing motives that lead to indecisiveness or avoidance (e.g., "I can't decide whether I will go on to graduate school until I know whether I'm getting married").

- Value, interest, or ability conflicts. For example, "I would love to be a teacher, but the salary isn't enough to support a family."

- Conflicts with significant others (e.g., "I want to be an interior designer, but Dad wants me to go into medicine, and I don't want to disappoint him").

- The struggle to control the future even though predicting the future is not possible.

- A tendency toward chronic procrastination because you don't know how to carry out the decision.[3]

- Mental health or medical issues. Depression, anxiety, grief, chronic pain, and the sudden onset of a medical illness can impair your ability to make a career decision. Depending on the severity of the mental health or medical issue, you may need to work closely with a mental health profession, physician, psychiatrist, or counselor to manage your symptoms in addition to working with a career counselor.

When making a career decision, carefully evaluate the costs, risks, and both the positive and negative aspects of each occupation. Many people make poor career choices because they really didn't understand what they are getting into. Other people allow family members or situations to dictate their decisions rather than making decisions themselves. There is no shortage of opinions in the world. Anyone can tell you what to do, but *you* will be the one who has to live with that career decision.

Making an Informed Career Choice

Most students aren't ready to declare a major simply because they do not have enough information to make a good career decision. Given today's economic conditions, many of you may want to know what the economic return will be on your college investment. You may be wondering what kind of job you can expect to find with a major in English, for example; how much you will earn after graduation and the potential job growth over the next decade. These are all important factors that go into making a good career decision.

Ideally, your career decision will be based on your personal interests, values, abilities, and personality style plus your research of current/future labor market trends.

Your goal is to make an informed decision based on the facts and backed up by your feelings. Here are some tips for making an informed career decision.

1. **Know yourself.** Be able to identify your strengths, talents, interests, personality style and motivations. Be realistic about your abilities. Self-knowledge is the key to being able to choose a career (and by default, a major) that will compliment who and what you are.

2. **Define success.** What does success or happiness mean to you (not to your parents, your friends, or your teachers)? What does a full filling life look like to you? How do you know when you'll be happy? What is more important to you (family, money, achievement, creativity, helping others, etc.)?

3. **Read the fine print.** Don't just follow the latest fad or go into a career because someone else thinks it's great. Narrow down your choices and then research what a person does in that career, all day and every day. What are the plusses and minuses of that job? What skills, education, licenses, or certifications are required to be successful in that that field? Do those requirements match your interests and abilities? Will you have the interest or persistence to complete the requirements of that field? Will you have the economic resources? If not, are there any alternatives that you can take to reach the same career or type of job?

4. **Look at the data.** Base your decision on up-to-date employment statistics, information, descriptions, and advice. Understand the employment situation for your chosen career. How are the employment prospects in your geographic area? What about salary (entry, mid, and upper levels)?

Will it be enough to live on? What would you need to do to increase your chances of employment or increase your earnings in that field? Use a financial aid loan calculator and a website like PayScale.com or Salary.com to run the figures against one another and see if the jobs you might get after graduation will cover the cost of the loans you take out. The goal is to put not put yourself in a position where you cannot repay your student loan expenses.

5. **Constraints.** Motivation has to do with how badly you want a particular career and how hard you are willing to work to reach your goal. Are you willing to spend the necessary time, money, and effort to complete the academic and postacademic requirements necessary to reach your career goal? Do you have family responsibilities that will factor into what type of major you choose? Are you limited geographically? The answers to those questions may affect your career choice.

Be actively involved in the decision-making process. Make a commitment that you *will* make a career decision (even though you may wish someone would do it for you). Be positive that you will be able to find a major, and career that will make you happy and support the type of lifestyle that you desire.

When you have made your career decision, ask yourself:

- Do I feel like I made the right career choice?
- Do I feel positive about my career choice?
- Do I feel confident that I can achieve my career goals?
- Does this career align with my interests, core values, abilities, and personality style? Approach this question from a different perspective and ask yourself, "What can I offer an employer?"

When you decide on a major that fits both objectively and subjectively, chances are that you've made a good career decision. A part of good strategic career planning is to periodically reassess your situation to make sure the direction you have chosen is still the one in which you want to continue. And always remember to remain open to new opportunities.

Always Have a Backup Plan

What should you do if the career you love happens to be competitive to get into, has fewer job prospects, or doesn't pay very well? Not everyone who dreams of becoming a professional athlete actually makes it (although some certainly do).

If, after having all of the facts, you decide to stick with your passion, or your dream career, then you'll need to do what it takes to make it work. This may mean that you'll have to the following:

1. Do additional internships or volunteer to gain experience to increase your chances of getting a job after college.
2. Move to where the jobs are. You can always move back home and get a job when you have more experience.
3. Get a job that will pay the bills (waitressing, retail) while you work on developing your real passion. When it develops enough to support you, quit the day job.
4. Pursue Plan B. You may just find that you enjoy your Plan B career more than or just as much as your original career. You can still continue to pursue your real passion at night, on the weekends, or in the summers (if you teach). You can always incorporate your passion into your live in another way: as a hobby, part-time moonlighting job, on weekends.
5. Find a related career that contains the same elements as your original career. If you love helping people but can't become a doctor, look for another career that has a strong element of helping others in a medical setting (medical imaging, dental hygiene, speech pathology, even psychology). If helping others is a prime interest, then consider counseling, teaching, human resources, and customer service. The O*Net online can help you dissect occupations according to skill and work environments.

Having a backup plan isn't a new idea. I was first introduced to the concept in college when I attended a freshman preveterinary major orientation class. The professor opened up the session by talking about something that none of us wanted to hear—namely, how difficult it was to become a vet, the percentage of students who wouldn't make it, and how we should all have a backup plan (blah, blah, blah). I, like many of my classmates, promptly dismissed the professor's remarks. Today, as a career counselor (note that I did *not* become a veterinarian), I completely understand why students are reluctant to consider alternative careers—because it means that they might have to give up their dreams.

So let's look at the situation in another way. Just because you decide not to pursue a particular major doesn't mean that you have to eliminate that passion from your life. If you love dancing, for example, but do not have what it takes to be successful on a professional level, you can still incorporate dance into your life by performing on an amateur level, teaching dance, attending dance performances, or joining a civic organization that promotes dance in your community. Many people, especially artists, make the decision to earn a living at their "day job" while pursing what they really love on the weekends.

Pursue your interests, but also do your research and make good choices for yourself. That way, you won't be surprised when you graduate. This is your opportunity to design the kind of life that you want. With all of the career options in the world today, you should be able to find something that you enjoy *and* be able to make a living. The key is to have the facts and then make an informed decision.

Write a Personal Mission Statement

Now that you've preliminarily (or definitely) decided on a major, articulate your short-term and long-term goals by writing a personal career mission statement. Your mission statement can be as long or as short as you like. Examples include "Become a best-selling science fiction author," "Complete my bachelor's degree in special education and secure a position working with autistic children," or "Earn my CPA and work for a large public accounting firm before opening a private practice in downtown Chicago."

Making a Career Plan

Using the results of your research into yourself and about your chosen major or career, you should be able to develop an educational plan that will enable you to reach your career goal. Enlist the help of your academic advisor. Use your career plan like the GPS in your car—as a way to track your progress toward your degree program. You can track your progress and know exactly what courses and requirements are still needed at any point along your career plan.

Include the following in your career plan:

- A summary of the type of college degree, work experience, and skills and attributes needed to enter your chosen career
- Name of college or university (the name of the college that you are attending, or plan to attend. For two-year college students, will you need to transfer to another school to complete a bachelor's degree?)
- Name of your major
- Type of degree (AAS, AS, BS, BA)
- The courses required (major, electives, minor? double-major?)

- Additional activities you will need to complete (volunteer experience, job shadowing, internships, co-op, membership in clubs and organizations)
- Certifications or licenses required
- Is graduate or professional school required?
- GRE or other graduate entrance examinations and application to other colleges/universities or graduate schools
- Cost, sources of funding (scholarship, grants, loans, etc.)
- A description of your ideal professional job (Refer to the results of your self-assessment and "Questions to Ask Yourself" in Chapter 11.)
- Your short-term and long-term career goals

Test Your Decision

After you have done all of your research, it's time to actively get involved in your career decision-making by *experiencing* your career in some manner. Reading about what a physical therapist does will only get you so far. Some people, like Herminia Ibarra, the author of *Working Identity: Unconventional Strategies for Reinventing Your Career*, believes that the best way to find your purpose and passion is by *doing*. She writes, "We learn who we are in practice, not in theory, by testing reality, not by looking inside."[4]

The next step is to give your career decision a test-run by taking courses in your intended major, doing an internship, a service learning project, a summer job, or volunteering. When you're finished, reevaluate your decision and repeat the process if needed.

Take Classes

Based on the information you have gathered and analyzed, you're ready to start taking classes to prepare yourself for your intended major. After you complete a few "major" courses, you'll start developing a better idea of your particular area of focus or concentration in your major.

Internships

For college students, there is no better way to "test-drive" a career than to experience it first-hand through an internship. Internships are a win-win. You get to experience your major in a supervised, real-world experience with a company while earning college credits. And you may even get paid for the experience. In return, the company can decide if they'd like to hire you on a permanent basis after you graduate. That's why internships are such a great idea (and why many college majors require one). Even if the internship doesn't lead to employment, at the end of the experience you will have learned some new skills and gained some valuable insight into your intended career. As a bonus, you can now add that experience to your resume. Hopefully, you will have been able to cultivate some professional relationships that can be used for future employment references.

Today, internships are one of the best ways college students can find a job upon graduation. A 2013 survey from The National Association of Colleges and Employers (NACE) revealed that students who completed a paid internship were more likely to get a job offer than someone who did their internship for free.[5] Many academic programs at the baccalaureate level now expect students to have more than one internship to be competitive in the marketplace after graduation.

(*Note*: If you are in a trade or career training program like automotive, welding, HVAC, nursing, dental assisting/hygiene, culinary, and so on, it will not be necessary to complete an internship. Your program's curriculum will automatically include hands-on classes and labs that are designed to provide on-the-job training and experience.)

Volunteer

Volunteering or completing a service-learning project in your major is a great way to get a feel for what that career will entail. When it comes to choosing a major, doing some volunteer work can help you learn which educational path is the one for you.

You may have done some volunteer work in high school as a way to make your college application stand out or to become more competitive when applying for scholarships. Now use volunteering to learn more about a career of interest. A secondary benefit of volunteering is that you'll have something to put on your resume to make your employment application stand out. Volunteerism also suggests that you're a team player, a quality many employers will look for in potential hires. Volunteer positions are a great way to network, especially if you volunteer in an area that is related to your future career. Interested in early childhood education? Try volunteering at a local daycare center or tutoring high school students during the summer. Even if you don't get anything else out of the experience, you will definitely know whether or not you want to pursue that profession. Check out Appendix A for a list of volunteer organizations.

Network

Networking continues to be the best job search method. It is estimated that 70 to 80 percent of all jobs are acquired through some form of networking. Students who intern with a company will naturally build relationships with supervisors and coworkers that can later turn into invaluable networking contacts. Use LinkedIn to connect with people in a job that you might like. Then ask your contacts for information about their job, the company they work for, and their career path up to that point. Another successful way to network is by joining a student chapter of a professional organization in your major. Then attend their meetings and begin making contacts with professionals in your intended field.

Try It Out for a Week

It's important to make sure you are going to like what you'll be doing for the next 40 plus years. Dedicate some time to "test" out your career idea by treating it as a job. As was mentioned earlier, do a summer job, volunteer, or internship in your major. The experience will help you decide if this is the career for you. Review and reflect on your decision at various intervals. Is it still a good decision? If not, begin the process again. People make adjustments in their career path all the time—and there's nothing wrong with that. It's just part of the decision-making process.

Changing Majors

Many students choose a major based on what they think it's going to be. Then they get into their first major class and, to their dismay, realize it wasn't what they thought at all. The best piece of advice that I received in college was, "You can always change your major." It's not uncommon to suddenly find out that you are headed down the wrong academic path. Lots of students do last-minute career changes based on a course that fell flat the previous semester.

Julie

Julie, a sophomore transfer student from another college, told me that she originally majored in nutrition because she was interested in helping people lead a healthier lifestyle. Unfortunately, she was very disappointed to find out there was so much chemistry involved in her major. So she switched her major to education because she really enjoyed her teachers in her senior year in high school. But after a couple of education courses, she found out that she didn't like her education major at all. Julie finally came in for career counseling. The results of her inventory surprisingly showed a surprising interest in business. She tried some courses and found that she really enjoyed the fast-paced, team-oriented aspects of marketing. Julie had finally found her niche.

Some Final Questions to Ask Yourself

1. Will I find this job interesting? Can I see myself doing this job all day? For several years?
2. Do I have the ability to earn the degree or complete the training that's required for this career?
3. How do my abilities and skills fit the tasks necessary to succeed in this career or profession?
4. Do I have the motivation to complete the courses and requirements needed to enter this career?
5. Will the working conditions and people suit me? How well does this work environment match my personality style? How happy or unhappy will I be under these work conditions?
6. Is this career consistent with my values and beliefs? How?
7. Will this career allow me to grow personally and professionally?
8. Will this career provide the rewards and satisfaction that I want in my life? Why?

If you answered "yes" to any of these questions, make sure you can cite solid reasons to support your answer. Likewise, if you answered "no" to any of these questions, understand why you answered the way you did. Is there an alternative way to approach or design this career so that it will meet your needs? Do you need to combine several careers? Finally, if what you love to do is not a feasible career possibility, can you adopt it as a hobby or "avocation" and choose something else that will allow you to economically survive?

Discuss your results with your parents, a friend, teacher, or advisor to make sure you are considering all factors. If you find you answered "no" more times than "yes," then consider discarding this career choice as a possible career or occupation. If this is the case, then you have made a good decision at this point in your life. Select another career or occupation and continue with your investigation.

Remember that your career plan is just a guide. It can be modified at any point in time. Reflect back at the end of the semester—do you need to revise your major or should you continue? Although it's difficult to make a decision based on only a handful of classes, the reality is that you will constantly be tweaking your career after graduation, when you get your first job, and your next job and after that. That's the way the process works and why we call it career development "across the life span."

CHAPTER FOURTEEN

What to Do When You're Stuck

We cannot become what we need to be by remaining what we are.
—Max De Pree

"I don't want to waste my time taking courses I don't need."
"I don't want to make the *wrong* choice."
"I want a job that will allow me to live comfortably but I just don't know what that is."
"I'm so confused right now that I just don't know what I want!"

Do any of these statements sound familiar? You want to find the right career but are so overwhelmed that you find yourself obsessing over the issue until you become mentally paralyzed. Even though you may endlessly discuss it with your friends and family, you find that you are no closer to making a decision.

"I come up with lots of ideas but then keep thinking of all the reasons why I don't want to do them," said Sandra, a third-semester student.

Often we struggle with making career decisions because we imagine that one choice is better than another; we have a fear of getting it wrong—trying something and failing at it, so we put pressure on ourselves to get it "right." Putting pressure on ourselves to *make* a decision inhibits creativity and interferes with our natural decision-making process. One student told me that she felt so much pressure to make a decision that she felt like she had the "weight of the world on her shoulders." When you start feeling that way, step back, take a deep breath, and understand that what you're going through is a *process*, not a once and done lifetime choice. Remember that you're not marrying your career. If you do make a career choice, it will not be etched in indelible ink—you can always change your mind. Sometimes you can't know if a major is right for you until you try it. If you try it out and find that it is not for you, then you can take this valuable information and adjust your path.

If you find yourself in a state of mental paralysis, shift your focus to your body. How do you feel emotionally and physically? Do you feel open, light, and relaxed or tense, heavy and stiff? Your body holds the answers if you learn to tune in and listen to it.

A simple method that I've used with students who are having a really hard time coming up with a major that they like is to eliminate the things that they *don't like*. Take the college catalog (or print off a list of majors that your college offers) and quickly go down the list and cross out the majors that you're not interested in. What's left are possible majors.

Choosing a career isn't one single ginormous decision. If you can view it as a process rather than a single earth-shattering event, you can break it down into a series of smaller step-by-step decisions that will be less scary and overwhelming. And, in the end, everything will work out for the best.

Antonio

Antonio was a first-year undeclared student who was really having difficulty coming up with what he wanted to do for a career. I asked him to write down what he *didn't* want to do. This is what he came up with:

- I'm terrible at writing papers.
- I can't stand to be around sick people.
- I can't sing and can barely draw a stick figure.
- While I liked playing sports and was on the baseball team in high school, it's not something that I want to pursue professionally.
- I'm not interested in anything automotive or electrical.
- I do not want to be a teacher.
- Computers are okay, but I don't want to sit in front of one all day.

After eliminating art, communication, English, journalism, health care, education, sports, and computer science majors, Antonio was left with business, engineering, and science. Business still involved quite a bit of writing, but, after taking an introductory business class, he realized that he did not have any interest in the subject material. Antonio researched the different types of engineering, but none of them appealed to him. So finally he decided to look at the science majors that the college offered: chemistry, biology, physics, and math. Antonio had always been good in science and math in high school. He took an introductory physics class, loved it, and realized that he had finally found his major.

Unsticking Common Scenarios

After working with undecided students over the years, I've come across some difficult, but common, scenarios. Here are some tips to help out even the most indecisive decision-maker:

1. **I hate everything**. Often, you'll see a low, flat profile on an interest inventory (i.e., no strong interest in any area). These are tough situations. Are any emotions such as anger or frustration overshadowing the issue? How do you feel about school in general? (One student told me that she hated school because they made her read books she didn't like.) You may have to seriously consider if college is the best option for you right now.

   Strategy: Go back to the basics and uncover at least one interest (everyone likes something, don't they?) Or, if all else fails, what can you major in that is at least tolerable? Can you complete *something* (even if it's in general studies or liberal arts and sciences), get a job after graduation, and then figure it out later?

2. **I like everything**. This is actually a good scenario because you have *options*. Some people have several equally strong interests. Portland-based Emilie Wapnick was like that. She founded Puttylike.com in 2010, an online resource for people who have many passions and creative pursuits. In an inspiring TED Talk, Wapnick explained that "multipotentialites" are not wired to pursue a single, overriding passion and devote their life to it. Instead, what really interests them is having the freedom to explore a dynamic range of jobs and interests over the course of a lifetime. In the past, these people were known as Renaissance Men. Examples include Leonardo da Vinci, Benjamin Franklin, and Thomas Jefferson.[1]

   Strategy: What do you want to do first? Can you combine your varied interests by double-majoring or minoring? Perhaps you're the type of person who needs to engage in several jobs and projects at the same time to satisfy your diverse interests? What about choosing one or two interests for a job and enjoy the others as hobbies? Or complete one major and then attend graduate school to pursue another? Sometimes the issue is a fear of having to "give up" something that you enjoy. By pursuing multiple interests in a combination of jobs and hobbies or in a series of careers, you won't have to "give up" anything.

3. **I just can't decide between two majors**. This situation often involves two disparate passions such as art and science.

Strategy: Can you combine both interests through creative majoring or minoring? Can you combine both passions into one occupation (e.g., art + biology = medical illustration)? Can you choose one interest for your "day job" and the other for a weekend job or a hobby? You don't necessarily have to give up either—just find a way to pursue both.

4. **I only want to do one thing.** Normally, this type of situation is not a problem unless (a) the major is "unacceptable" (i.e., parents don't think you'll get a job) or (b) you were academically dropped or denied entry into major. Explore why you are so focused on this one major—is it lack of exposure to other options? An overriding passion for a particular career? Pressure to go into the "family business?"

    Strategy: In the case of lack of career exposure, work with your advisor or career counselor to explore new interests, try out different types of courses, and learn a little bit more about yourself, before making a career choice. Most career fields have similar or related jobs that can be just satisfying and rewarding. If you can't be a neurosurgeon but still enjoy medicine and helping others, there are plenty of other related health-care careers that contain these traits: radiology, physical or occupational therapy, speech pathology, physician assistant, chiropractic, and so on. Once you have clearly defined what you are looking for in a career, you will find that there are a number of paths that match those criteria.

    If you are totally fixated on becoming a nurse, for example, and was not accepted into the nursing program, here are some options: (a) look at other ways to become a nurse (different school, first become LPN and then an RN), or (b) after some more self-exploration, can you find another occupation that will allow you to satisfy your desire to help people or your interest in working in a medical environment? Get some tips from your career counselor on how to discuss the issue with your parents and work on reframing any underlining career myths (e.g., viewing career unrealistically and using that career as a way to enhance self-esteem)

    Lastly, in the case of being denied entrance into major, you may need sufficient time to go through the grieving process. Can you take a semester off? Develop a "backdoor" plan to reach your goals? If none of these options are possible because of educational or financial time restraints, at least understand that you're going through a grieving process and try to come up with some Plan B's (warning: I know this sounds easier to do than it really is).

5. **I'm just too overwhelmed to decide.** This means you've been trying too hard to make a decision.

    Strategy: Lighten up and release the pressure to make a decision *right now!* Break down the process into manageable steps. Reframe any negative self-talk about "I *have* to make a choice," or "I'm choosing a major for the *rest of my life.*"

6. **I'm afraid of choosing the "wrong" major.** I hear this one a lot. You may have been told, directly or indirectly, not to waste time and money in college by changing majors. Or perhaps you are very concerned about finding a career that will adequately support you and a family in the future.

   Strategy: Depending on the source of the issue, your options are the following:

   a. Reframe the myth that there is one, "perfect job."

   b. Understand that there are no "wrong" choices because it's all about becoming educated, and so on.

   c. Pursue your interests, yet be selective about your employment choice to maximize your earning potential.

   d. Reframe the notion that you are "stuck" with your career choice. Remember that this is just a starting point. You can always change your major or your job.

   e. Can you become more comfortable with being "undecided?" Having control over a future that you can't predict is almost impossible. Allow some time to help you sort out things. (This is a tough one, I'll admit. Not everyone is comfortable with happenstance theory.)

7. **I don't know what I like.** Sure, you do. You're just feeling too overwhelmed right now.

   Strategy: Your goal is to uncover your "secret" interest. Often the issue is that what you love is not an acceptable career choice for you or your parents (e.g., art, photography). Find out what you'll need to do to find employment or the value of developing a Plan B. Lastly if don't know what you like because you are not aware of your interests and abilities, then begin with an interest inventory to gain some valuable insight about yourself.

Danielle Flug Capalino, MSPH, RD, described her circuitous career path in a recent blog. Danielle had two great loves—fashion and the brain. Even though her family had been in the fashion business, they convinced her to pursue science. After finishing a degree in neuroscience at the Massachusetts Institute for Technology, she went to work in the fashion industry. During her research at MIT, she became aware of the registered dietician profession.

Danielle wrote in her blog, "I came to realize during this journey that fashion and science really weren't so different. There were a few common threads: decision-making and behavioral change, that I really wanted to explore."[2]

MIT did not have an RD program, so Danielle eventually completed courses at three different schools before finishing her degree in a combined program at John Hopkins.

In my work as a career services director, I spend a lot of time assuring students that what they're going through is perfectly normal. Even though they lament that "all of my friends know what they want to do," I tell them that there are plenty of other students (about 50%) who are feeling just as confused as they are.

CHAPTER FIFTEEN

Unique Circumstances

The future belongs to those who believe in their dreams.

—Eleanor Roosevelt

College can be difficult, even in the best of circumstances. College presents even greater challenges for students who have unique life circumstances such as age, family responsibilities, physical or medical issues, or learning disabilities.

Adult Students

Adult students come in all ages and circumstances. Some are individuals who have been the victims of downsizing and are now forced to reevaluate their lives and look at other options. Others are women facing a pending divorce or who are recently divorced and need to get back into the workforce (or enter it for the first time). Still other adult students are those who stopped out of college for one reason or another and have elected to reenter and finish their degree.

Adult students begin college with more fears and concerns than traditional-aged students. Both groups worry about finding a major they'll like, the length of time it will take to graduate, and whether or not they'll be able to support themselves after graduation. Traditional-aged students face uncertainty about their careers and future but, unlike adult students, have the advantage of time and sometimes even the advantage of money. Adult students have the additional complications of age, family, and financial responsibilities. They are concerned about making their mortgage payments on time, balancing family and school, and a myriad of other responsibilities that most 18-year-olds have yet to experience. Most adult students are considered "independent," under financial aid guidelines, and may have to work full time while they're attending school just to make ends meet.

Some adult students went straight into the workforce after their high school graduation and are now trying to make the adjustment back into academia. They may feel that their brains are bit rusty and their computer skills out-of-date. Others are single parents trying to juggle school and home in an attempt to make a better life for themselves and their children.

Values seem to play a greater role in adult student's career decision-making. For some, a new career can mean a fresh start or the chance at a better life. Some of the motivation behind going back to school may deal with the larger life issue of creating a more fulfilling or meaningful life. Many students, young and old alike, choose careers based on money, power, and status. Yet, recently, there's a trend toward creating lifestyles that have meaning and make a contribution to the world. Other adult students want to take the opportunity to resurrect former career aspirations or rectify missed opportunities or decisions made in the ignorance of youth. I can't tell you how many adult students have told me, "If I only knew *then*, what I know *now*, I would have _____."

Issues Adult Students May Face

- Highly motivated, but may be impatient to finish their degree
- Worry about fitting in and being successful
- Have financial and family responsibilities that may interfere with class and study time
- May need remedial skills training
- May not be up to date on resume and job search techniques
- May have a priority of finishing school and finding a good-paying job in the shortest amount of time

As an adult student you may feel that you do not have the luxury of being able to pursue your dream of becoming a chiropractor, for example, because of the time and expense involved. You may be deliberating between pursing the career you most enjoy and completing one that can be completed in a shorter time frame and get you out into the workforce more quickly. When I work with adult students who are hesitant to pursue a bachelor's degree because they think it will take too much time (even though it may pay more in the long run), I ask them to consider this: the time is going to go by anyway, so why not use it to reach your dreams? Four or five years from now you're going to look back and say, why didn't I just go for my degree in education, or [you fill in the blank]?

Some students elect to go to school on a part-time basis, at night, or on the weekends and work during the day, or vice versa. Others make the decision to leave their job, apply for financial aid, or borrow money from a relative in order to go to school full time. There are plusses and minuses to both scenarios. You'll have to sit down and weigh the costs and benefits of each type of strategy to determine which will work best for you.

Single Parents

Single parents have been described as "having twice the responsibility but only half the income." Many single parents, men and women alike, go to school in hopes of being able to create a better life for their children. Some of the biggest concerns facing single parents are having limited financial or social support, and having adequate or affordable child care. Time management is a huge issue, as it is for any adult student who has to balance work and home responsibilities. College courses generally require more time and effort than high school classes. Some single parents may be forced to go part time just to be able to get their kids to and from school and take care of their own needs. Trying to get everything done may leave time only for homework after the kids go to bed, which is why many single parents end up not getting enough sleep, which ends up creating its own set of problems. Going part time increases the length of time spent in school, which may increase the overall cost of attendance (tuition only goes up, not down) and ultimately delays the financial benefit gained from being in the workforce.

Your choice of major really depends on your interests and how long you want to go to school. Many single parents are focused on completing a degree that will lead to a stable, well-paying job, such as nursing. Looking at associate degree programs (e.g., accounting, business) that "step up" to bachelor's degrees may also be good options. You'll be able to get a job after two years and then have the option of continuing your education at night or online if you choose to do so. Many single parents find that they are freer to complete a bachelor's degree or graduate work once their children are in school.

Janice

Janice was a 28-year-old single parent of a 3-year-old daughter. Her reason for attending college was very clear: "My motivation for going back to school is my daughter—I want to be able to give her a good life," she said.

Janice spent the first year at college completing the prerequisite courses for the respiratory therapy associate degree program. She took many of the courses online so she could be available to take her daughter to day care. Because Janice was receiving welfare benefits, she qualified for a special program that helped her with some of her extra expenses like travel costs to school and clinical uniforms. When she was accepted into the respiratory therapy program, Janice's mother and her aunt took turns picking up and watching Janice's daughter after day care on the days that Janice's respiratory clinical ran later than 5:00 p.m. It was a difficult struggle to juggle homework and family responsibilities, but Janice eventually completed her degree, landed a good-paying position at a nearby hospital, and was able to get off of welfare.

Unemployed

Most people are emotionally unprepared for job loss and find it devastating when it does happen. Many experts compare the emotional effects of job loss with a grief reaction. The problem is that most employees are asked to make significant decisions about their future without the necessary time to process what has just happened. Many of the individuals I see need to make a relatively quick decision about whether to go back to school or find another job. Many, however, are still in the midst of the shock, anger, or depression stages of their grief. Ideally, the "acceptance" stage is the place to be when determining what you want to do with the rest of your work life. Unfortunately, many displaced employees simply do not have the luxury of waiting until they reach this point.[1]

There may be compounding grief or anger issues that may interfere with the ability to make a career decision (or any decision) at this point in time. There may be conflicting decisions about whether to go back to school or go out and find a job. A referral may be needed to the unemployment office, or for credit counseling. Depending on the funding situation, there may be immediate need to make career decision.

Explore all options (e.g., retrain or find employment), prioritize needs, and create short-term and long-term goals. Some unemployed individuals actually experience a sense of relief at being laid off—it now gives them the opportunity to do something different (or better) with their lives.

Recently Divorced or Widowed Students

If you are newly divorced or widowed and have spent the past several years staying at home to raise your children and manage the household, it has probably been many years since you last worked, not to mention attended school.

Some of you may have an immediate need to support yourself by finding a part-time job or upgrading your computer skills to gain employment. You may want to prioritize your needs and create short-term/long-term goals.

Similar to unemployed students, grief or anger and the immediate need to earn a living may interfere with or limit the time you have to choose a major. It may be prudent to develop a Plan A: obtain basic skills to obtain immediate employment such as computer skills and a Plan B: find employment and then continue furthering your education through an employer's tuition reimbursement program.

Career Changers

There are two types of career changers: voluntary (wish to change careers because of dissatisfaction or boredom with current job or career) and involuntary (forced to change careers because of injury or illness).

Voluntary career changers face many of the same challenges that adult students in general face: family, financial, and time constraints. When choosing a new career, it is important to do your research. You will want to investigate salary, job openings in your local geographic area, and the amount of time and resources required to reach your new career goal. A career change is generally easy to accomplish if your new career is somewhat related to your previous career or job because transferrable skills and experience can be utilized. The downside to making a career change to an entirely new career is the amount of time it will take to earn your new degree and the fact that you will be starting at an entry-level wage when you graduate. The good news is that career changers generally move up the proverbial career ladder more quickly because of the benefit of their prior years of work experience.

Involuntary career changers face the added complication of dealing with the loss of a profession or job that they may have really enjoyed. Voluntary career changers are happy to change careers—but this may not necessarily be the situation in an involuntary career change situation. I recently worked with a dental hygienist who had to give up a profession that she really enjoyed because of chronic back and shoulder pain—an occupational hazard from bending over clients and cleaning teeth all day. Involuntary career changers need to find a new occupation that will support themselves.

For those of you who can no longer physically continue in your job or profession because of injury or an accident, your emotional reactions are going to be similar to the person who has suddenly been laid off because you have experienced a sudden, unexpected termination from your career. However, unlike the person who has been laid off, you do not have the option of continuing to your former job at a new place of employment. You will have to find a new job or profession, which essentially forces you to reinvent yourself. You may find that your career options are limited because of your health or physical limitations; you may be experiencing grief and/or anger over your physical limitations and loss of your occupation. Finally, time and money may still be an issue even though your schooling may be funded through a government agency like Vocational Rehabilitation or Social Security Disability.

LGBTQ Students

While it is true that some fields may be more restrictive about how open a person can be about his or her sexual orientation (e.g., elementary education, criminal justice, or the military), the truth of the matter is that LGBTQ people are employed and have been successful in a variety of occupations.[2]

The growing acceptance of homosexuality in the United States has encouraged many LGBTQ individuals to "come out" before or during their college years. In an article in *Academic Advising Today*, Brandy Smith writes, "The "coming out" process may include student discomfort with sexual orientation and may lead students to choose careers that are traditionally seen as congruent with gender stereotypes."[3] Asking yourself why you want to choose a particular major can indicate how satisfied you're going to be if your choice was made because of gender stereotypes. Ms. Smith writes, "Some persons may be satisfied with choosing a career path based upon gender stereotypes, but others may realize that alternative reasons for choosing a major may be more important."[4] When considering possible careers, your task will be to challenge commonly held stereotypes and assumptions and broaden your list of career possibilities instead of limiting the majors to stereotypical fields. Some interest inventories, like the Strong Interest Inventory, are normed for gender. When taking the Strong Interest Inventory, answer the questions based on your *identi-fied* gender.

There are a number of LGBTQ organizations that can provide networking and support for students and graduates such as Out Professionals (www.outprofessionals.org) and the Human Rights Campaign (www.hrc.org). Work with your career center, or your school's GLBT organization to identify LGBT friendly employers in your area and learn about strategies to deal with possible discrimination in the interview and workplace.

Students with Special Needs

It is important to recognize that being a person with a disability does not equate to having a lack of capacity—but rather a gap between your strengths and the environment. To be successful in college, you will need to develop additional competencies to navigate postsecondary education and the transition to employment.[5]

Strategies for academic success:

- Make sure that you understand your rights and responsibilities as an individual with a disability.
- Use your school's resources and team up with your accessibilities coordinator, academic advisor, and career center and any other professional as appropriate.
- Find, request, and secure supports and accommodations along with an understanding of their use, not only in an academic environment but also how they may be adapted to a work-based environment.
- Work with your career center to explore career options.
- Work with your career center and your advisor to determine when and how to disclose one's disability in different situations.

If you are a student who has Asperger's Syndrome, try to choose a career that capitalizes on your interests and unique strengths. Consider environmental "fit" and the degree of interpersonal communication that is required when making a career decision. Look beyond basic career descriptions and read actual job descriptions to determine if the work environment will be most conducive to your success.

Barbara Bissonnette, principal of forward motion coaching, specializes in career development coaching for individuals with Asperger's Syndrome. She says,

> If you have Asperger's Syndrome (autism spectrum disorder), think twice about choosing a college major or job based solely on your interests.

Although you may be fascinated with a topic such as history, or passionate about books, you may not enjoy or be able to manage the jobs that are available in those areas. For example, librarians spend considerable time interacting with the public. If you are a prospective major in library science, think about your comfort level when meeting new people. Some fields, such as museum archiving, have few job openings. It can take a significant amount of networking to find employment.

Bissonnette advises, "Before deciding on a course of study or a job, do the following:

- Identify the specific jobs related to your area of interest. What are the primary tasks? What skills are needed to complete those tasks? How easy will it be for you to acquire those skills?

- Determine the type and amount of interpersonal interaction that is required. Can you tolerate interacting with other people for most of the day, or you need to work independently?

- Examine the work environment. How fast is the pace? Are there frequent interruptions? Will there be sounds, odors, or other sensory stimuli that would be distracting or unbearable?"

According to Ms. Bissonnette, "Databases such as the *Occupational Outlook Handbook* (www.bls.gov/ooh/) provide useful overviews of various jobs. However, they do not explicitly explain duties and aspects of the work environment that are considered "obvious" to people who are not on the autism spectrum. Get help from a family member, teacher, or professional who can translate abstract terms such as self-starter, team player, and "good" people skills."

Ms. Bissonnette suggests, "Although individuals are represented in all types of jobs and careers, the fields of computer technology, academic and scientific research, writing, engineering, technical documentation, and academia may be good choices because they can capitalize on your logic and analytical skills, attention to detail, and ability to focus for extended periods of time."[6]

Veterans

Many newly released veterans find the transition back into civilian life to be a challenge, for a variety of reasons. Now add going to school and choosing a major. Take the time to carefully think about what you'd like to do with your life from this point on. Were there any parts of your military occupation that you really enjoyed, and would like to continue to do? What about any career aspirations that you had before you entered the military? Many veterans want to continue to serve or protect in some manner. If that's the case with you, then work with your career counselor or coach to find a career that captures those characteristics.

Veterans' values often change, sometimes drastically, as a result of their military service. Many realize after they are discharged that they are different people, especially if they have experienced combat.[7]

Most veterans are not traditional-aged college students; they've had significant life experiences prior to enrolling in college. Because many veterans have spouses and/or children, families are an important consideration when deciding to pursue a certain career.

When you were in the military, many of your career decisions (and decision in general) were made for you. You now have the opportunity to make your own career decisions. Explore different options before committing to a new career choice. Discuss the impact of any service-related disability or subsequent mental health issue may have on your career decision.

Student veterans bring with them real-world experience and, in many cases, strong leadership and teamwork skills. One of the challenges some veterans face is being able to translate their military skills into civilian terms. Eighty-one percent of military jobs have a civilian equivalent.[8]

The following are links to free military to civilian "translators" you can use to make the connection to civilian jobs.

- http://www.military.com/veteran-jobs/skills-translator (provided by Military .com and powered by Monster)
- http://www.careerinfonet.org/moc/default.aspx?nodeid=213 (provided by the U.S. Department of Labor, Employment and Training Administration)
- http://www.onetonline.org/crosswalk (provided by O*NET online, includes apprenticeships, education, and translators)

Students with Criminal Records

A felony on your record can greatly limit your career choices. The exact list of occupations and types of restrictions depend on your offense and state and federal regulations. Even students who have a prior common misdemeanor, such as a DUI, may be denied entrance into a health-care or early childhood education program.

In general, it is illegal for employers to refuse to hire you just because you have a criminal conviction; however, you can be barred from working in a job that is related to your conviction.[9] "Barred Occupations," a career planning article for people with criminal convictions, provides some examples:

- "If your offense was related to alcohol, it is legal for an employer to stop you from working in a liquor store, or as a server in a restaurant that sells alcohol.
- If your offense was related to firearms, you can be barred from working in places that sell guns. You also cannot work in security and law enforcement occupations that require you to be near weapons.
- If your offense was related to money, you can be barred from working in a bank or other financial institution."[10]

Occupations that require a license may not be open to someone who has a felony. Examples are the following:

- Health-care occupations, such as nurses, counselors, professional engineers, and certified public accountants
- Occupations that work with children
- Occupations that serve the elderly or adults with special needs[11]

The article goes on to say, "Some organizations, like nursing homes, will help you to obtain a license so you can work there. This is why it is a good idea to make connections with employers. You want to be considered based on your qualifications and personality, not your criminal record."[12]

Although the limited number of career options can be discouraging, there are still plenty of options to choose from:

- Advertising
- Art
- Automotive/diesel mechanics
- Carpentry
- Communications
- Computer information systems or technology
- Construction
- Culinary, pastry arts, food preparation
- Customer service sales (except pharmaceutical sales)
- Drug and alcohol counselor

- Electrical or electronics engineering technology
- Entrepreneurship
- Graphic design typing, data entry, administrative assistant (may depend on the employer)
- Landscaping
- Language translator
- Marketing
- Plumbing, HVAC (commercial, not residential)
- Truck driving
- Warehousing
- Welding
- Writing

Remember that time is your best friend. Some jobs and workplaces have a 7-, 10-, or 15-year limit on restrictions. It is important to never lie about your criminal record because your record will be revealed through a preemployment background check. To assure employers that you have moved on from your past activities, openly admit regret for the activities and provide examples of how you have moved on with your life, such as returning to school and earning your degree.

Your goal in college is to establish a solid work record references of people who can vouch for your employability and character. This can be accomplished through part-time or volunteer work, clinicals, and internships.

Students Who Have Been Denied Entrance into Major

While some students quickly realize they need to change their career plans, some students experience a career crisis arise after a forced realization (failing grade, probation, rejection letter). I have observed that the degree of "crisis" depends on the competitiveness of the major, the amount of emotional energy invested in a career plan, the degree of parental involvement, and what the pending career loss means to the student. If you have been denied entrance into your major, it is helpful to remember that you will be experiencing a grief reaction to the *loss* of your career dream. Some of you, especially those of you in health-care majors, are very passionate about what you perceive as your life's "calling" and can be especially devastated by the prospect of abandoning your career goals.

Your goal will be to work with your advisor or career center to find another path to reaching your goal, even if that means transferring to another school, or finding another profession that you will enjoy just as much. A related health-care profession might be just as enjoyable.

For some students the situation becomes worse when they tell their parents. Although most parents react with sympathy and support, some react with anger or disappointment. First-generation college students often carry the hopes and dreams of generations before them. Others are expected to follow in their parent's footsteps or achieve their parent's unrealized goals or aspirations. This places a tremendous amount of pressure on students to succeed. To some students, loss of the major means loss of their parent's love and support.

It is important that you understand *why* you were not accepted into a program so you can use that knowledge to make sound future choices. It is often difficult to see the "larger picture" and understand the incremental nature of skill acquisition or why academic standards are required for certain professions.

Here are some steps to help you recover and move on:

Stop negative language. Refrain from labeling yourself as "stupid" or a "failure." There is no shame in trying something even if the outcome was not successful. Work with your career counselor to use language to describe the situation in a way that will retain self-esteem and interpret failure in a way that facilities success in the future.

Generate options. Is it possible to retake a course, retake an entrance exam, or reapply to a program? Is there another academic route that would lead to the same career? Does another institution offer the same program? Is there a related or similar major that you would be interested in pursuing?

Deal with parents. Talk with your career counselor or academic advisor about how you believe your parent(s) will react. Most parents are simply worried that you won't be able to support yourself. Role-play scenarios. Practice using language to explain the situation to your parents.

Career counseling. Work with your career center to identify your interests, strengths, and values and apply them to other career areas. Make sure to do your research. You don't want to inadvertently set yourself up for failure by not realistically accessing your abilities, by not following your true passions, or by underestimating the academic rigor of a program. What initially attracted you to this major? Are there other related, but less competitive majors that would be equally satisfying?

Time. In my experience, some students are too emotionally devastated to be able to focus on choosing another major. Part of the "crisis" in these situations arises from having to make immediate decisions about changing majors, dropping courses, withdrawing from school, or applying to another program. Take some time off (holiday or summer break) to grieve, reflect, and consider other career options.

Although this may feel like a hopeless situation, it is not the end of the world. You will be able to continue your education and become successful in another area.

CHAPTER SIXTEEN

Are You Career Ready?

Success is peace of mind that is the direct result of self-satisfaction in knowing you did your best to become the best that you are capable of becoming.

—John Wooden

To get the most out of career planning, it's important to understand what exactly you are planning for. The terms "career," "job," and "occupation" are often used interchangeably, although they are actually quite different.

A *career* is a series of work experiences, usually in the same area, that are pursued over a person's lifetime. A career encompasses more than income and benefits; it is a lifetime progression of using your skills, education, knowledge, and experiences.

A *job* refers to a specific position within an occupation. A job sometimes implies a source of paid income or what you do for a living, not necessarily who or what you are.

An *occupation* is a category of jobs that are grouped together because of similar characteristics.

Getting Ready for Career Success

Many graduates assume that completing their degree is all that is needed to be successful in the professional world. But employment trends are influenced by the current economic climate. The availability of jobs in your geographic area will determine the ease or difficulty of your job search. If you recently earned a highly sought-after degree where there are more job openings than applicants, then you probably won't have too much trouble finding a job. In fact, recruiters will probably come to you.

In a poorer job market (more applicants than positions), finding a job becomes more competitive and usually takes much longer. To maximize your chances for success, you should rely more on networking and use multiple methods for finding job openings. If your major does not require an internship, clinical, practicum, student teaching, or some other form of practical work experience, you should still consider doing one. An internship bridges your classroom experience with the real world of work. It cannot only be listed on your resume, but many employers prefer to hire students directly from internship experiences.

When should you start looking for a job? In general, you should start looking for advertised job openings, making contacts with recruiters and potential employers, and attending job fairs and employer information sessions as early as possible in the semester that you plan to graduate. And don't forget to register with your career center—they receive hundreds of job openings from employers every semester.

Remember that having a good resume will help your search immensely, but the resume will only get you in the door. After that, how well you conduct yourself in the interview will ultimately determine if you're hired.

The Importance of Soft Skills

In the work world, skills are important to an employer—sometimes even more important than your degree. Skills are things that you can do. Some skills are job specific and can be used in only one line of work, like being able to interpret an X-ray. Skills that can be used in several occupations are known as "transferrable skills." Examples of transferrable skills are providing good customer service, word processing, or being able to write a report. You may have developed these skills in school and on the job, from volunteering or through life experiences.

We often hear employers talk about "soft" skills and "hard" skills. Soft skills are a combination of your personality, attitude, and social skills and do weigh heavily in an employer's decision to consider you as a candidate. Candidates with poor soft skills are an employer's worst nightmare. Examples are employees who are unreliable, argumentative, self-serving, unmotivated, or dishonest or just have terrible attitudes. Unlike hard skills, soft skills are broadly applicable both in and outside the workplace. These are the skills you need to enter, stay in, and progress in the world of work. Examples of soft skills are the following:

- Communication
- Problem solving

- Positive attitude
- Motivation
- Adaptability
- Working well with others
- Being organized
- Working well under pressure
- Having a strong work ethic

"Hard" skills (also known as technical skills) are the career-specific skills and knowledge that you learn in your college classes. In general, hard skills refer to a person's skill set, education, training, and the ability to perform a certain type of task or activity. Examples of hard skills are the following:

- Running computer software programs
- Fixing machinery
- Operating equipment
- Performing laboratory procedures
- Being proficient at interviewing clients
- Using a specific teaching method

Hard skills are usually easier to demonstrate than soft skills. However, some employers believe that soft skills are more important in the long run than hard skills. Hard skills alone are not enough to land a job in many companies—you will also need soft skills to land, and keep, a job.

Regardless of your major, every graduate will need to demonstrate his or her soft and hard skills to a potential employer when looking for a job. In today's competitive job market, you will need to articulate the value of your skills and degree to a potential employer to land the job. The resume is the first step in the job-hunting process to establish that connection. To be successful in today's competitive job market, your resume and cover letter must be action-driven and clearly demonstrate the value that you will bring to a company.

These are examples of skills that employers particularly look for and how to demonstrate them in the interview.

- **Strong work ethic**. How hard are you willing to work to get the job done? Prove that you have a strong work ethic by giving past examples illustrating how you went "above and beyond" to get a job done.

- **Positive attitude**. Are you optimistic and upbeat? Will you generate good energy and good will? Smile when you shake the interviewer's hand, and look and sound like you're interested in the position.

- **Effective communication**. Good verbal and written communication skills are important in almost every occupation and include articulating oneself well, being a good listener, and using appropriate body language. In the interview, provide examples of written reports, campaigns, or other written examples or be able to talk about examples of giving speeches, and so on.

- **Time management abilities**. Do you know how to prioritize tasks? Can you effectively manage your time to work on multiple projects? Use examples from group projects in class, volunteer positions, running meetings, and membership in student clubs and organizations.

- **Self-confidence**. Do you truly believe that you can do the job? Do you inspire confidence in others? You can demonstrate self-confidence during the interview by the way that you carry yourself, answer questions, greet others with a firm handshake, and good eye contact and by sitting upright rather than hunching over.

Transferrable Skills

Transferrable skills are skills that you learn in one setting but can apply in another setting. Answering the telephone, writing a report, and being well organized are all examples of transferrable skills. Organizing or public speaking are examples of transferable skills that can be used in any workplace setting, while skills like accounting or drafting are more applicable to specific settings.[1]

Most college students have a difficult time seeing how the skills they learned in college will transfer to the workplace. We all have skills, just by virtue of living. Transferrable skills are often acquired through classroom projects and assignments or experiences such as campus organizations or activities, athletic activities, hobbies, internships, fieldwork experiences, practicums, clinicals, internships, and summer or part-time jobs.

Transferable skills are skills that all employers look for in a potential hire. Consider them as a complement of your academic degree. In a resume, transferrable skills are identified by action verbs like "performed," "wrote," "supervised," "coordinated," "developed," and "performed." When you apply for a job, analyze the job description to determine which skills the employer has prioritized. Then provide proof to an employer that you possess that skill in a cover letter, in resume, or in an interview by providing specific examples of how you successfully used your organizational skills in the past.

Here's an example:

Local law firm has an entry-level opening for a paralegal for a litigation practice. Hours are 11:30 a.m. to 8:00 p.m. Salary commensurate with experience. Paralegal certificate and/or Bachelor's Degree and strong computer and Internet skills, including experience with Microsoft Office Suite, are required. Excellent research and communication skills required. Full health benefits, 401k and parking included. Excellent work environment. All replies strictly confidential.

After reading the job description, pull out the skills required by this employer and then illustrate, with examples, how you possess those skills. Use examples from your college coursework, extracurricular activities, and past employment:

- Paralegal certificate and/or bachelor's degree (earned a bachelor's degree in paralegal studies from American University)
- Strong computer and Internet skills (proficient in Microsoft Office 2016, Windows 10—earned an "A" in CIS 101)
- Excellent research skills (experience performing pretrial document research using Lexis during a summer internship at a local law firm)
- Excellent communication skills (earned grade of "A" in speech communications 100 class; previous customer service experience from part-time position as customer service representative at ABC Company interacting with customers and resolving problems in person and over the phone)

Remember that transferable skills supplement the knowledge you have gained from your degree, making you a more competitive job candidate.

Professionalism

You've heard how important it is to be professional if you want to be a success. But what exactly does "being professional" mean? Professionals can be defined as individuals who are expected to display competent and skillful behaviors in alignment with their profession. Being professional is the act of behaving in a manner defined and expected by the chosen profession.

In addition to acting the part, professionals have to *look* the part. In other words, they are dressed appropriately for the situation and carry themselves with poise and confidence. It is important to earn a professional reputation in the workplace. True professionals are often the first to be considered for promotions and are regarded by others as being successful in their careers.

Why is professionalism important in the job search? Students who are not able to make the transition from college to the workplace are at a huge disadvantage in the job market. In the interview, first impressions are crucial. Not dressing or behaving appropriately, or professionally, can really make you stand out—and not in a good way. In addition to being dressed appropriately, body language, eye contact, grammar, and mannerisms all contribute to professionalism. Even your voice mail and e-mail address can signal professionalism (or the lack of) if it's inappropriate. An employer recently told me that he passed on bringing in one of our graduates for an interview because the student had an obnoxious, and very unprofessional, voice mail message.

Here are just a couple of basic tips to create a positive and professional first impression in the interview.

- Be prompt and courteous.
- Smile and be gracious and friendly to everyone you meet.
- When a hand is extended, smile and shake hands firmly.
- Enunciate and avoid using slang or unprofessional language.
- Do not chew gum or smoke.
- Do not turn on or check your cell phone.
- Do not become unduly familiar or relay private or personal information about yourself other than casual comments about extracurricular activities, hobbies, or interests. And always keep the conversation focused on work and school.

It's also important to maintain a positive, professional image online. Search for your name online and see what comes back in the results. Remove any questionable posts and images form your social media pages (Facebook, Twitter, LinkedIn).

Think about people in your life whom you consider professional. How do they dress? How do they speak? How do they handle themselves in difficult situations? How do you want to be viewed in your professional career?

Career Readiness

The jobs of the future will continue to require more education and training than they did in the past. Jobs that require only a high school diploma are quickly disappearing.

Employers and educators have been engaged in long discussions to ensure that our educational system is aligned with our workforce needs. In 2015, the National Association of Colleges and Employers, through a task force of college career services and HR/staffing professionals, developed a definition of "career readiness" and identified seven competencies that are critical in preparing college graduates for a successful transition into the workforce.[2] In January 2017, they added an eighth competency.

These competencies are the following:

1. Critical thinking/problem solving
2. Oral/written communications
3. Teamwork/collaboration
4. Information technology application
5. Leadership
6. Professionalism/work ethic
7. Career management
8. Global/intercultural fluency

To read more about career readiness and the eight career competencies, go to: http://www.naceweb.org/knowledge/career-readiness-competencies.aspx.

Job Searching Advice for New Graduates

My advice to graduates is to look for employment early and often, be creative, and utilize a variety of different sources for job leads. Here are some tips to help new graduates find jobs in any type of economy:[3]

- **Start early.** It's important to begin the job search process *before* you graduate, not after. Don't fall into the trap of telling yourself that you'll look for a job after you get through finals—that's what everyone else will be doing. In a tight economic market you should begin looking early because it may take longer than anticipated to find a position. Register with your career services office and attend job fairs. Once you've secured a position, you can relax and enjoy the remaining months of school.

- **Network**. Networking is by far the best way to find employment. Talk to family, friends, neighbors, professors, other professionals, and anyone else you know who can help you locate job openings. Who knows, you might even hear about a job before it's advertised.

- **Volunteer or complete internships.** In today's job market, internships and volunteer assignments often lead to permanent positions. Take advantage of any part- or full-time employment opportunity, paid or not, just to gain valuable job experience and references. Understand that you will be competing for jobs not only with fellow graduates but also against other job seekers who have more work experience.

- **Widen your geographic radius.** Consider searching for and applying for openings in locations that you wouldn't otherwise consider because you think they are "too far away." Gas prices have come down dramatically, which will help offset commuting costs. Do not be afraid to go where the jobs are located.

- **Stress results on resumes and in interviews.** Employers want to know what you have *done*. Highlight any accomplishments from internships, coursework, clinicals, or field experiences. Use a portfolio in the interview to illustrate examples of your accomplishments.

- **Be flexible and strategic.** In highly competitive industries, you may have to take a job that isn't your first choice. Use that opportunity to build skills while continuing to look for other opportunities. Sometimes you have to take a job at a slightly lower salary than originally hoped for just to get the experience. This doesn't mean that you have to stay at that job forever or at that salary level. Remember, when you're just starting out in your career, having *a* job in your major is better than having no job at all.

How to Ensure Future Marketability

In today's workforce, you are in charge of your career. While this can be an exciting prospect, it also means that you will need to keep an eye on the marketplace and constantly upgrade just to survive.

Here are some strategies to survive and thrive in the new workplace of the future:

- **Keep your skills updated**. Many professions require that members continually complete professional development courses to remain current in their fields. This can be accomplished through a variety of ways such as attending conferences and webinars, taking undergraduate or graduate classes, obtaining new certifications, renewing licenses, and reading professional journals. Likewise, many companies sponsor professional development opportunities, so take advantage of them. People in health-care or technology careers especially need to keep up with new developments or quickly become obsolete.

- **Continue to network**. Many of us become so comfortable within our own circle of expertise that we lose our connections with the outside world. This actually makes us less secure because we are less aware of changes and, conversely, opportunities, and as a result we become less marketable in the long run. Stay in contact with professionals in your field, former employers, and former colleagues or clients. These people are an invaluable source of referrals, new ideas, contacts, and information about the future.

- **Keep a record of your accomplishments**. Update your resume once a year and make sure to add any professional development activities, training, courses, volunteer work, new skills that you have acquired, and the results of projects or assignments. Also, keep copies of performance reviews or evaluations.

- **Add value at work**. Be productive and go above and beyond your basic job responsibilities. Volunteer for extra assignments, learn additional job responsibilities, or act as a backup for other positions in your department. In the event that positions are slated to be eliminated at your company, you may be able to quickly step into another position within your organization.

- **Review and set goals once a year**. Use this time to review the past year. Many professionals will routinely do this when submitting an annual report to their boss. Review your personal and professional accomplishments. Ask yourself, what have I accomplished this year? What do I need to accomplish the following year? Are there any skills that I need to learn or improve upon? If I lost my job today, would I be able to successfully find another? If not, what would I have to do to become more marketable?

- **Be aware of current events in your industry**. Stay abreast of any trends that may affect your profession. This is where talking to outside professionals may help by providing you with valuable outsider information. Being able to spot future trends not only will give you time to prepare for a position shift in the event of a corporate merger, layoff, or change in company mission but will ensure that you will not be caught off guard.

- **Keep an eye open for possibilities**. Some people routinely scan job openings just to keep up on what's out there in the marketplace. Opportunities present themselves to people who are open to receiving them. This is where joining professional organizations or the "groups" feature on LinkedIn comes in handy because it helps you stay current with the newest ideas, issues, and events happening in your profession. When the time comes, you will have all of the resources necessary to make a transition.

When all is said and done, the way that you conduct yourself on the job will be key to your career success and future employability. Employers want people who are hardworking and agreeable and who bring value to the organization. Keep your boss apprised of what you have been doing and what you have accomplished—don't rely on him or her to know your worth.

Career experts say that the art of self-promotion, especially in a supervisory or management position, is one of the main reasons some people are promoted and others are not.[4]

The science (and art) of managing your career begins with your first part-time job or internship in college and continues until retirement. As you move through life, you will continue to improve your skills; add to your experiences; and upgrade your career in terms of advancement, better pay, more responsibility, better working conditions, and more job security. You may continue to follow your original career path or, like many of us, suddenly change directions, depending on the circumstances. Many of us will work well into, and past, retirement age or begin new careers when we retire. You will spend the majority of your waking hours working in whatever career you choose—so choose wisely and enjoy the journey.

Volunteer Organizations

Local Volunteer Organizations

Community service clubs (Boy Scouts/Girl Scouts, 4-H, Lions clubs, Kiwanis, Jaycees, the Shrine, Rotarians, etc.)

Political parties (League of Women Voters, Democratic Party, Republican Party, Tea Party, Libertarians, etc.)

Churches (feeding the homeless, Sunday school and bible study teachers, missionary work)

Schools (tutoring, teacher's aides, crossing guards)

Hospitals (gift shop, admissions, switchboard, deliver mail and flowers, visit patients, etc.)

Law enforcement (escort women, rape prevention, provide transportation, etc.)

Volunteer fire and emergency services departments

Hospices and nursing homes (visit patients, lead group activities, fundraising)

Cultural organizations (fund-raising, building sets, selling tickets, acting, supervising outings for children, etc.)

Recreational organizations (coaches, referees, umpires, score keepers, etc.)

National Volunteer Organizations

Action against Hunger (http://www.actionagainsthunger.org)

American Association of Retired People (http://www.aarp.org)

American Cancer Society (http://www.cancer.org)

The American Red Cross (http://www.redcross.org)

AmeriCorps/Vista (http://www.nationalservice.gov/programs/americorps)

Appalachian Trail Conservancy (http://www.appalachiantrail.org)

The Arc (http://www.thearc.org)

Best Friends Animal Society (http://bestfriends.org)

Big Brothers/Big Sisters (http://www.bbbs.org)

Boy Scouts of America (http://www.scouting.org)

Catholic Charities (http://catholiccharitiesusa.org)

Chesapeake Bay Foundation (http://www.cbf.org)

Christian Children's Fund (http://www.christianchildrensfund.org)

Department of Veteran's Affairs (http://www.volunteer.va.gov)

Doctors without Borders (http://www.doctorswithoutborders.org)

Dress for Success (http://www.dressforsuccess.org)

Feed the Children (http://www.feedthechildren.org)

Food for the Hungry (http://www.fh.org)

Girl Scouts (http://www.girlscouts.org)

Global Volunteers (http://www.globalvolunteers.org)

Habitat for Humanity (http://www.habitat.org

The Humane Society (http://www.humanesociety.org)

Idealist (http://www.idealist.org/ip/volunteerOpportunitySearch). Also known as "Action without Borders"

Keep America Beautiful (http://www.kab.org)

League of Women Voters (http://lwv.org)

Make a Wish Foundation (http://www.wish.org)

March of Dimes (http://www.marchofdimes.org)

Meals on Wheels (http://www.mealsonwheelsamerica.org)

National Coalition for the Homeless (http://www.nationalhomeless.org)

National 4-H Council (http://www.4-h.org)

National Mentoring Partnership (http://www.mentoring.org)

Oceanic Society (http://www.oceanic-society.org)

1–800-VOLUNTEER.org (http://www.1-800-volunteer.org). Provides direct connections to local volunteer opportunities that match interests and skills.

Operation Smile (http://www.operationsmile.org)

Orangutan Foundation International (http://www.orangutan.org)

Peace Corps (http://www.peacecorps.gov)

Rainforest-Alliance (http://www.rainforest-alliance.org)

Save the Children (http://www.savethechildren.org)

Sierra Club (http://www.sierraclub.org/outings)

St. Jude's Children Research Hospital (http://www.stjude.org)

The United Way (http://www.unitedway.org)

Volunteer.gov (http://www.volunteer.gov) Natural and Cultural Resources Volunteer Portal

Volunteer Travel (http://www.volunteertravel.com)

Volunteers for Peace (http://www.vfp.org)

Wildlife Conservation Society (http://www.wcs.org)

Professional Organizations

Accounting

American Accounting Association (http://www.aaahq.org)

American Institute of Certified Public Accountants (http://www.aicpa.org)

The Association of Accountants and Financial Professionals in Business (http://www.imanet.org)

National Society of Accountants (http://www.nsacct.org)

Actuarial Science

American Academy of Actuaries (http://www.actuary.org)

Casualty Actuarial Society (http://www.casact.org)

Society of Actuaries (http://www.soa.org)

Administrative Professionals

Association of Executive and Administrative Professionals (http://theaeap.com)

Advertising

American Advertising Federation (http://www.aaf.org)

American Association of Advertising Agencies (http://www.aaaa.org)

Agronomy

American Society of Agronomy (http://www.agronomy.org)

Animal Science

The American Society of Animal Science (http://www.asas.org)

Architecture

The American Institute of Architects (http://www.aia.org)
National Kitchen & Bath Association (http://www.nkba.org)
Society of Architectural Historians (http://www.sah.org)

Astronomy

American Astronomical Society (http://www.aas.org)

Athletics

National Athletic Trainers' Association (http://www.nata.org)
National High School Athletic Coaches Association (http://www.nhsca.com)
National High School Basketball Coaches Association (http://www.nhsbca.org)

Audio and Visual Communications

The National Association of Broadcasters (http://www.nab.org)
Radio Television Digital News Association (http://www.rtdna.org)
Society of Broadcast Engineers (http://www.sbe.org)
Society of Camera Operators (http://www.soc.org)

Automated Manufacturing

The Association for Manufacturing Technology (http://www.amtonline.org)

Automotive Technology

Automotive Service Association (http://asashop.org)

Aviation

Airline Pilots Association (http://www.alpa.org)
National Business Aviation Association (http://www.nbaa.org)

Banking

American Bankers Association (http://www.aba.com)

Independent Community Bankers of America (http://www.ibaa.org)

Biochemistry

American Society for Biochemistry & Molecular Biology (http://www.asbmb .org)

Biology

American Institute of Biological Sciences (http://www.aibs.org)

American Society for Biochemistry and Molecular Biology (http://www.asbmb .org)

American Society for Cell Biology (http://www.smbe.org)

The Ecological Society of America (http://www.esa.org)

Society for Integrative and Comparative Biology (http://www.sicb.org)

Botany

American Society of Plant Biologists (http://my.aspb.org)

Botanical Society of America (http://www.botany.org)

Business

American Business Women's Association (http://www.abwa.org)

American Management Association (http://www.amanet.org)

National Business Association (http://nationalbusiness.org)

Society of Human Resource Management (http://www.shrm.org)

U.S. Small Business Association (http://www.sba.gov

Chemistry

American Chemical Society (http://www.acs.org)

Chiropractic

American Chiropractic Association (http://www.acatoday.org)

Clinical Laboratory Science

American Society for Clinical Laboratory Science (http://www.ascls.org)

Association of Clinical Scientists (http://www.clinicalscience.org)

Commercial Art

American Institute of Graphic Arts (http://www.aiga.org)

National Association of Independent Artists (http://www.naiaartists.org)

National Cartoonists Society (http://www.reuben.org)

Professional Association of Visual Artists (http://pava-artists.org)/

Professional Photographers of America (http://www.ppa.com)

Wedding & Portrait Photographers International (http://www.wppionline.com)

Communication

American Communication Association (http://www.americancomm.org)/

International Speech Communication Association (http://www.synsig.org)

National Communication Association (http://www.natcom.org)

Computer-Aided Drafting and Design

American Design Drafting Association (http://www.adda.org)

Computers/Information Technology

The American Society for Information Science and Technology (http://www.asist.org)

Association for Information Technology Professionals (http://www.aitp.org)

IEEE Computer Society (http://www.computer.org)

Construction/Building Industry

American Society of Heating, Refrigerating and Air Conditioning (http://www.ashrae.org)

Associated General Contractors of America (http://www.agc.org)

Building Service Contractors Association International (http://www.bscai.org)

The Masonry Society (http://www.masonrysociety.org)

National Concrete Masonry Association (http://www.ncma.org)

National Insulation Association (http://www.insulation.org)

Court Reporting

National Court Reporters Association (http://www.ncra.org)

Criminal Justice

Academy of Criminal Justice Sciences (http://www.acjs.org)

Culinary Arts

American Culinary Federation (http://www.acfchefs.org)

Cyber Security

American Society for Industrial Security (http://www.asisonline.org)

Dental

American Dental Association (http://www.ada.org)

Dental Assisting

American Dental Assistants Association (http://www.adaausa.org)

Dental Hygiene

American Dental Hygienists Association (http://www.adha.org)

Drafting

American Design Drafting Association (http://www.adda.org)

Education

American Association of School Administrators (http://www.aasa.org)

National Association for Family and Community Education (http://www.nafce.org)

National Association of Secondary School Principals (http://www.nassp.org)

National Education Association (http://www.nea.org)

Electrical/Electronics

Institute for Electrical and Electronic Engineers (http://www.ieee.org)

National Electrical Contractors Association (http://www.necanet.org)

Emergency Medical Services

American Ambulance Association (http://www.the-aaa.org)

National Association of Emergency Medical Technicians (http://www.naemt.org)

Engineering

American Academy of Environmental Engineers (http://www.aaees.org)

American Institute of Chemical Engineers (http://www.aiche.org)

American Nuclear Society (http://ans.org)

American Society for Engineering Education (http://www.asee.org)

American Society of Civil Engineers (http://www.asce.org)

American Society of Mechanical Engineers (http://www.asme.org)

The Architectural Engineering Institute (http://www.asce.org)

Institute of Electrical and Electronic Engineers (http://www.ieee.org)

National Society of Black Engineers (http://www.nsbe.org)

National Society of Professional Engineers (http://www.nspe.org)

Society of Hispanic Professional Engineers (http://www.shpe.org)

Society of Women Engineers (http://www.swe.org)

Exercise Science/Fitness

American Society of Exercise Physiologists (http://www.asep.org)

National Health and Exercise Association (http://www.nhesa.org)

Fire Science

International Association of Firefighters (http://www.iaff.org)

Forestry

Society of American Foresters (http://www.eforester.org)

Genetics

American Society of Human Genetics (http://www.ashg.org)
Genetics Society of America (http://www.genetics-gsa.org)

Geography

Association of American Geographers (http://www.aag.org)

Geology

American Geophysical Union (http://www.agu.org)
American Institute of Professional Geologists (http://www.aipg.org)
Association for Women Geoscientists (http://www.awg.org)
Geological Society of America (http://www.geosociety.org)

Horticulture

American Horticulture Society (http://www.ahs.org)
American Public Gardens Association (http://publicgardens.org)
National Gardening Association (http://garden.org)

Hospitality

American Hotel & Lodging Association (http://www.ahla.com)

Human Resources

National Human Resources Association (http://www.humanresources.org)
Society for Human Resource Management (http://www.shrm.org)

Human Services

American Public Human Services Association (http://www.aphsa.org)
National Organization for Human Services (http://www.nationalhumanservices.org)

Humanities

American Philosophical Society (http://www.amphilsoc.org)
Humanities Education and Research Association (http://www.h-e-r-a.org)

Interior Design

American Society of Interior Designers (http://www.asid.org)
International Interior Design Association (http://www.iida.org)

Journalism

American Society of Journalists and Authors (http://www.asja.org)
Society of Professional Journalists (http://www.spj.org)

Landscape Architecture

American Society of Landscape Architects (http://www.asla.org)
Association of Professional Landscape Designers (http://www.apld.org)

Law

American Bar Association (http://www.americanbar.org)
American Health Lawyers Association (http://www.healthlawyers.org)
American Intellectual Property Law Association (http://www.aipla.org)
Association of Child Abuse Lawyers (http://www.childabuselawyers.com)
National Association of Criminal Defense Lawyers (http://www.nacdl.org)
National Network of Estate Attorneys (http://www.netplanning.com)
The Sports lawyers Association (http://www.sportslaw.org)

Legal Assisting/Paralegal

National Association of Legal Assistants (http://www.nala.org)

Library Science

American Library Association (http://www.ala.org)
Medical Library Association (http://www.mlanet.org)

Marine Biology/Oceanography

Association for the Sciences of Limnology and Oceanography (http://aslo.org)

Marine Technology Society (http://www.mtsociety.org)

Marketing

American Marketing Association (http://www.ama.org)

Market Research Association (http://www.marketingresearch.org)

Massage Therapy

American Massage Therapy Association (http://www.amtamassage.org)

Mathematics

American Mathematical Society (http://http://www.ams.org)

Mathematical Association of America (http://www.maa.org)

National Council of Teachers of Mathematics (http://www.nctm.org)

Medical Assistant

American Association of Medical Assistants (http://www.aama-ntl.org)

Medical Imaging

American Registry of Magnetic Resonance Imaging Technologists (http://www
.armrit.org)

American Society of Radiologic Technologists (http://www.asrt.org)

Association for Medical Imaging Management (http://www.ahraonline.org)

Society of Diagnostic Medical Sonography (http://www.sdms.org)

Medical Reimbursement & Coding

American Health Information Management Association (http://www.ahima.org)

Medicine

American College of Sports Medicine (http://www.acsm.org)

American Medical Association (http://www.ama-assn.org/ama)

American Medical Women's Association (http://www.amwa-doc.org)

Meteorology

American Meteorological Society (http://www.ametsoc.org/ams)

Mortuary

National Funeral Directors Association (http://www.nfda.org)

Motorsports

American Racing Club (http://www.ncracing.org)

International Motor Sports Association (http://www.imsa.com)

National Auto Sport Association (http://nasaproracing.com)

National Hot Rod Association (http://www.nhra.com)

Music

The American Society of Composers, Authors, and Publishers (http://www
.ascap.com)

Music Recording

The Society of Professional Audio Recording Services (http://www.spars.com)

Nuclear Engineering

American Nuclear Society (http://www.ans.org)

Nursing

American Nurses Association (http://www.nursingworld.org)

National League for Nursing (http://www.nln.org)

Nutrition

Academy of Nutrition and Dietetics (http://www.eatright.org)

American Dietetic Association (http://diabetes.org)

American Nutrition Association (http://americannutritionassociation.org)

Occupational Therapy

American Occupational therapy Association (http://www.aota.org)

Optometry

American Optometric Association (http://www.aoa.org)

National Optometric Association (http://www.nationaloptometricassociation.com)

Pastry Arts

American Society of Baking (http://www.asbe.org)

Pharmacy

American Association of Pharmaceutical Scientists (http://www.aaps.org)

American Pharmacists Association (http://www.pharmacist.com)

Physical Therapy

American Physical Therapy Association (http://www.apta.org)

Physician Assistant

American Academy of Physician Assistants (http://www.aapa.org)

Physics

American Institute of Physics (http://www.aip.org)

American Physical Society (http://www.aps.org)

Podiatry

American Podiatric Medical Association (http://www.apma.org)

Political Science

American Political Science Association (http://www.apsanet.org)

Psychology/Counseling

American Art Therapy Association (http://www.arttherapy.org)
American Counseling Association (http://www.counseling.org)
American Music Therapy Association (http://www.musictherapy.org)
American Psychological Association (http://www.apa.org)
Association for Applied Sport Psychology (http://www.appliedsportpsych.org)
National Association of School Psychologists (http://www.nasponline.org)
National Rehabilitation Counseling Association (http://nrca-net.org)

Public Relations

Public Relations Society of America (http://www.prsa.org)

Respiratory Therapy

American Association of Respiratory Care (http://www.aarc.org)

Social Work

National Association of Social Workers (http://www.socialworkers.org)

Sociology

American Sociological Association (http://www.asanet.org)

Speech Pathology and Audiology

Acoustical Society of America (http://acousticalsociety.org)
American Speech-Language-Hearing Association (http://www.asha.org)

Surgical Technology

Association of Surgical Technologists (http://www.ast.org)

Surveying

American Society for Photogrammetry and Remote Sensing (http://www.asprs.org)

National Society of Professional Surveyors (http://www.nsps.us.com)

Urban & Regional Information Systems Association (http://www.urisa.org)

Theater

American Association of Community Theatre (http://www.aact.org)

Screen Actors Guild (http://www.sag.org)

Therapeutic Recreation Therapy

American Therapeutic Recreation Association (http://www.atra-online.com)

Veterinary Science

American Veterinary Medical Association (http://www.avma.org)

North American Veterinary Technician Association (http://www.navta.net)

Web Development

Association of Web Design Professionals (http://www.awdp.org)

World Organization of Webmasters (http://webprofessionals.org)

Welding

American Welding Society (http://www.aws.org)

Wildlife

National Wildlife Rehabilitators Association (http://www.nwrawildlife.org)

Zoo/Aquarium

Association of Zoos and Aquariums (http://www.aza.org)

Helpful Career Resources

General Career Information Websites

America's Career InfoNet (http://www.acinet.org)
Your one-stop shop for career-related resources. Includes career videos and information about career exploration, salary, and occupational projections by state.

BigFuture (https://bigfuture.collegeboard.org/careers)
This website, created by the College Board, features an extensive section on college majors and careers.

Career Cornerstone Center (http://www.careercornerstone.org)
This extensive site explores over 185 degree fields in science, technology, engineering, mathematics, and medicine and offers detailed education requirements, salary and employment data, precollege ideas, and career planning resources.

Career Profiles (http://www.careerprofiles.info/careers.html)
Explore thousands of careers and occupations organized by field and specialty.

College Career Life Planning (http://www.collegecareerlifeplanning.org)
This noncommercial site provides access to more than 500 of the best, free, educational, and career planning tools on the web for college students, career changers, and job seekers.

Guidance Resources Home Page (http://www.wisemantech.com/guidance)
An excellent collection of web-based career resources developed by the former guidance director at Carl Sandburg High School. Select "Specific

Career Information" to learn about career opportunities in a variety of fields from animal behavior to paleontology.

My Next Move (http://www.mynextmove.org)
Sponsored by the U.S. Department of Labor, this site allows you to search careers by key words or by industry or connects you to the O*Net Interest Profiler.

O*Net (http://www.doleta.gov/programs/onet)
A complete tool for career exploration and job analysis. Includes occupational descriptions, employment projections, military transition search, and green careers. Published by the U.S. Department of Labor.

Job Search Websites

CareerBuilder (http://www.careerbuilder.com)
This nationwide job board allows you to search for job openings, post your resume, and receive listings.

CityTown Info (http://www.citytowninfo.com)
An excellent source of unique facts about cities across the United States. Also contains a career directory with an extensive set of employment data organized by both profession and city location.

Federal Employment (http://www.usajobs.com)
Federal employment information and resume builder.

GettingHired (http://www.gettinghired.com)
This site helps talented people with disabilities prepare for the work place and build their career.

Glassdoor (http://www.glassdoor.com)
Glassdoor.com gives you an inside look at company interview questions, salaries, and reviews, for thousands of companies.

Indeed (http://www.indeed.com)
A comprehensive job search engine providing free access to millions of jobs and internships from thousands of job boards, newspaper classifieds, and company websites.

Job Search USA (http://www.jobsearchusa.org)
Search for jobs anywhere in the United States by career or state.

LinkedIn (http://www.linkedin.com)
Best known as a professional networking social media site, LinkedIn allows you to post your resume (or a more informal, customized version), to link to other people's profiles, to participate in group discussion boards, and to publish posts. It also allows you to look up people who work in a given field or at a given company based on keyword searches.

LinkUp (http://www.linkup.com)
A job search engine that pulls jobs from company websites. All jobs are updated automatically. As a result, jobs are always current, often unadvertised anywhere else, and contain no fake jobs or scam listings.

Monster.Com (http://www.monster.com)
A monster-sized career site with something for job seekers at all stages of the job search.

Simply Hired (http://www.simplyhired.com)
An excellent job search engine that allows you to search for jobs, network, and research trends.

Employment Outlook Websites

Bureau of Labor Statistics (http://www.bls.gov/emp)
This site provides a wealth of employment information including employment projections for the next 10 years.

CityTown Info (http://www.citytowninfo.com/employment)
An excellent source of unique facts about cities across the United States. Also contains a career directory with an extensive set of employment data organized by both profession and city location.

Occupational Outlook Handbook (http://www.bls.gov/ooh)
A detailed source of information about hundreds of occupations.

Entrepreneurship

The Small Business Administration (http://www.sba.gov/
Resources from the small business administration for anyone wanting to start a small business.

Notes

Introduction

1. Catherine Taibi, "25 People Who Prove It's Never Too Late for a Career Change," *Huffington Post*, June 24, 2014, accessed September 19, 2016, http://www.huffingtonpost.com/2013/06/24/never-late-change-careers_n_3460618.html.

2. Leah Rozen, "Stand Up; Sit Down; Talk, Talk, Talk," *New York Times*, July 9, 2010, accessed September 19, 2016, http://www.nytimes.com/2010/07/11/fashion/11WITH.html?_r=2.

3. "Julia Child in the OSS," *Barry Bradford*, September 21, 2012, accessed September 19, 2016, http://barrybradford.com/julia-child-in-the-oss.

4. "Sheryl Crow," Biography.com, last updated August 18, 2016, accessed November 29, 2016, http://www.biography.com/people/sheryl-crow-9542181#synopsis.

Chapter 1. College Is a Major Deal

1. Bureau of Labor Statistics, "College Enrollment and Work Activity of 2015 High School Graduates," *Economic News Release*, accessed July 18, 2016, http://www.bls.gov/news.release/hsgec.nr0.htm.

2. Ibid.

3. Anthony P. Carnevale, Tamara Jayasundera, and Artem Gulish, *America's Divided Recovery: College Haves and Have-Nots* (Washington, DC: Georgetown University Center on Education and the Workforce, June 30, 2016), 15, accessed September 19, 2016, https://cew.georgetown.edu/cew-reports/americas-divided-recovery/#full-report.

4. Ibid.

5. Anthony P. Carnevale, Nicole Smith, and Jeff Strohl, *Recovery: Job Growth and Education Requirements through 2020* (Washington, DC: Georgetown University Center on Education and the Workforce, June 2013), 15, accessed July 18, 2016, https://cew.georgetown.edu/wp-content/uploads/2014/11/Recovery2020.ES_.Web_.pdf

6. Pew Research Center, *The Rising Cost of Not Going to College* (Washington, DC: Pew Research Center, February, 2014), accessed July 18, 2016, http://www.pewsocialtrends.org/2014/02/11/the-rising-cost-of-not-going-to-college.

7. "The Value of a College Degree," *Education Corner,* accessed September 19, 2016, http://www.educationcorner.com/value-of-a-college-degree.html.

8. Ibid.

9. College Board, "New College Board Trends in Higher Education Reports: College Prices Increase at a Slower Pace While Student Borrowing Declines for the Third Consecutive Year," *College Board Press Release,* accessed July 18, 2016, https://www.collegeboard.org/releases/2014/new-college-board-trends-higher-education-reports-college-prices-increase-slower-pace-student-borrowing-declines-third-consecutive-year.

10. Ibid.

11. Experience, Inc., "Career Statistics," Experience.com, 2016, accessed August 9, 2016, https://www.experience.com/alumnus/article?channel_id=career_management&source_page=additional_articles&article_id=article_1247505066959.

12. Ibid.

13. "Student Expectations and Preferences," *The Class of 2013 Student Survey Report* (Bethlehem, PA: National Association of Colleges and Employers, Winter 2016), 11–12.

14. Scott Jaschik, "Majoring in a Professor," *Inside Higher Ed,* August 12, 2013, accessed October 25, 2016, https://www.insidehighered.com/news/2013/08/12/study-finds-choice-major-most-influenced-quality-intro-professor.

15. Ibid.

16. David K. Moldoff, "Can't Decide on a College Major?," College Transfer.net, March 15, 2013, accessed August 9, 2016, accessed January 26, 2017, http://www.collegetransfer.net/ContinueMyEducation/ChangeSwitchTransfer/Iwantto/EarnMyCollegeDegree/TheUndecidedMajor/tabid/934/default.aspx.

17. John D. Krumbolz, "The Happenstance Learning Theory," *Journal of Career Assessment,* 17, no. 2 (2009): 135–154.

18. Virginia N. Gordon, *The Undecided College Student: An Academic and Career Advising Challenge,* 2nd ed (Springfield, IL: Charles C. Thomas, 1995), 59–63.

19. Yuritzy Ramos, "College Students Tend to Change Majors When They Find the One They Really Love," Borderzine.com, March 15, 2013, accessed August 9, 2016, http://borderzine.com/2013/03/college-students-tend-to-change-majors-when-they-find-the-one-they-really-love.

20. Complete College America, *Four-Year Myth: Make College More Affordable: Restore the Promise of Graduating on Time* (Indianapolis, IN: Complete College America, 2014), accessed July 18, 2016, http://completecollege.org/wp-content/uploads/2014/11/4-Year-Myth.pdf.

21. Ibid.

Chapter 2. How to Choose a Career

1. John L. Holland, *Making Vocational Choices: A Theory of Vocational Personalities and Work Environments*, 3rd ed. (Odessa, FL: Psychological Assessment Resources, 1997).

2. UC Davis Staff Development and Professional Services, "Holland's Occupational Themes," *University of California Davis*, last updated March 24, 2014, accessed February 1, 2017, http://sdps.ucdavis.edu/toolkits/career_manage ment/learnaboutyourself/self_assessments/hollands_occupational_themes .html.

3. John D. Krumbolz, "The Happenstance Learning Theory," *Journal of Career Assessment*, 17, no. 2 (2009): 135–154.

4. American Psychological Association, *Career Counseling with Mark Savickas*, video series, notes, 2006, accessed July 22, 2016, http://www.apa.org /pubs/videos/4310737.aspx?tab=2.

5. Lisa E. Severy, "What's My Story? Narrative Intervention in Career Counseling" (doctoral dissertation, University of Florida, 2006), 8, http://ufdc.ufl.edu /UFE0013422/00001/18j.

6. Jon Schlesinger and Lauren P. Daley, "Career Development Models for the 21st Century," *NACE Journal*, April 2016, accessed August 3, 2016, http://www .naceweb.org/knowledge/career-development-models-21st-century.aspx.

7. Spencer G. Niles, Norman E. Amundson, and Roberta A. Neault, *Career Flow: A Hope-Centered Approach to Career Development* (Boston: Pearson Education, 2011).

Chapter 3. Dispelling Common Career Myths

1. "Popular College Degrees and Programs," MatchCollege.com, 2016, accessed October 25, 2016, http://www.matchcollege.com/top-majors.

2. "Myths about Majors," University of La Verne website, accessed October 25, 2016, http://sites.laverne.edu/careers/what-can-i-do-with-my-major.

3. Yuritzy Ramos, "College Students Tend to Change Majors When They Find the One They Really Love," Borderzine.com, March 15, 2013, accessed August 9, 2016, http://borderzine.com/2013/03/college-students-tend-to-change-majors-when-they-find-the-one-they-really-love.

4. Jeanne Meister, "Job Hopping Is the 'New Normal' for Millennials: Three Ways to Prevent a Human Resource Nightmare," Forbes.com, August 14, 2012, accessed October 7, 2016, http://www.forbes.com/sites/jeannemeister/2012 /08/14/job-hopping-is-the-new-normal-for-millennials-three-ways-to-prevent-a-human-resource-nightmare/#736681535508.

5. "Career Statistics," Experience.com, 2016, accessed August 9, 2016, https:// www.experience.com/alumnus/article?channel_id=career_management&source_ page=additional_articles&article_id=article_1247505066959.

Chapter 4. Who Are You?

1. Sonja Lyubomirsky, *The How of Happiness: A Scientific Approach to Getting the Life You Want* (New York: The Penguin Press, 2007).

2. Rachel Suppok, "The Science of Extraversion and Introversion," Truity .com (blog), February 2, 2016, http://www.truity.com/blog/science-extraversion-and-introversion.

Chapter 5. Careers for Compassionate People

1. "Teacher Salary," Salary.com, as of December 28, 2016, accessed January 19, 2017, http://www1.salary.com/Teacher-salary.html.

2. "Average Salary for All Postsecondary Teachers, Professors, Associates, Assistants," Payscale.com, updated January 14, 2017, accessed January 19, 2017, http://www.payscale.com/research/US/All_Postsecondary_Teachers_%2F_Professors_%2F_Associates_%2F_Assistants/Salary.

3. "Is a Health Care Career Right for You?," *Diversity Matters*, November 11, 2016, accessed January 15, 2017, http://oursuperheroeswi.org/health-care-career-right.

4. Andrea Clement Santiago, "How to Become an Anesthesiologist," Verywell .com, Updated July 31, 2016, accessed January 15, 2017, https://www.verywell .com/how-to-become-an-anesthesiologist-1736304.

5. "Kinesiotherapist," ExploreHealthCareers.org, 2017, accessed January 15, 2017, https://explorehealthcareers.org/career/sports-medicine/kinesiotherapist.

6. "O& P Professionals," *OPCareers*, accessed January 15, 2017, http://www .opcareers.org/professionals.

7. Ibid.

8. "Surgeon Salaries," Salary.com, as of December 28, 2106, accessed January 19, 2017, http://www1.salary.com/Surgeon-salary.html.

9. "Health Physicist Salary," Payscale.com, updated October 28, 2016, accessed January 19, 2017, http://www.payscale.com/research/US/Job=Health_Physicist/Salary.

10. "Physician—Radiology Salaries," Salary.com, as of December 28, 2016, accessed January 15, 2017, http://www1.salary.com/Radiologist-salary.html.

11. "Occupational Therapist Salaries," Salary.com, as of December 28, 2016, accessed January 16, 2017, http://www1.salary.com/Occupational-Therapist-salary.html.

12. "Certified Occupational Therapy Assistant Salaries," Salary.com, as of December 28, 2016, accessed January 16, 2017, http://www1.salary.com /Certified-Occupational-Therapist-Assistant-salary.html.

13. "Ophthalmologist Salary," Salary.com, as of December 28, 2016, accessed January 19, 2017, http://www1.salary.com/Opthalmologist-salary.html.

14. ExploreHealthCareers.org, 2017, accessed January 15, 2017, http:// explorehealthcareers.org.

15. "Human Services Worker Salaries," Salary.com, as of December 28, 2016, accessed January 19, 2017, http://www1.salary.com/Human-Services-Worker-salary.html.

16. "Social Worker (BSW) Salaries," Salary.com, as of December 28, 2016, accessed January 19, 2017, http://www1.salary.com/Social-Worker-BSW-salary.html.

17. "Choosing a Career in Counseling," *American Counseling Association*, 2017, accessed January 15, 2017, https://www.counseling.org.

18. "Mental Health Counselor Salary," Payscale.com, updated January 12, 2016, accessed September, 21, 2016, http://www.payscale.com/research/US/Job=Mental_Health_Counselor/Salary.

19. "Psychology Salaries," Salary.com, as of December 28, 2016, accessed January 19, 2017, http://www1.salary.com/Psychologist-salary.html.

20. "Funeral Director Salary," Payscale.com, updated January 12, 2016, accessed September 21, 2016, http://www.payscale.com/research/US/Job=Funeral_Director/Salary.

Chapter 6. Careers for Analytical People

1. Scott M. Deitche, *Green Collar Jobs: Environmental Careers for the 21st Century* (Santa Barbara, CA: Praeger 2010), 18.

2. Rich Feller, "STEM: Where Are the Women?," StemCareer.com, May 23, 2016, accessed August 2, 2016, http://stemcareer.com/?s=stem%3A+Where+are+the+women%3F.

3. National Association of Colleges and Employers, *Winter 2016 Salary Survey* (Bethlehem, PA: National Association of Colleges and Employers, Winter 2016), 5.

4. National Association of Colleges and Employers, *Winter 2017 Salary Survey* (Bethlehem, PA: National Association of Colleges and Employers, Winter 2017), 4.

5. Dean Stallard, "What Skills Are in Demand in the Life Sciences Industry?," LinkedIn.com, July 19, 2016, accessed August 2, 2016, https://www.linkedin.com/pulse/what-skills-demand-life-sciences-industry-dean-stallard.

6. "Most New Jobs," *Occupational Outlook Handbook*, 2016–17 ed. (Washington, DC: U.S. Department of Labor, December 17, 2015), accessed August 2, 2016, http://www.bls.gov/ooh/most-new-jobs.htm.

7. "Career Opportunities as Mobile Apps Developer," Indcareer.com, January 16, 2015, accessed August 2, 2016, https://www.indcareer.com/article/308633/career-opportunities-mobile-apps-developer.

8. National Association of Colleges and Employers, *Winter 2017 Salary Survey*, 9.

9. "Mobile Applications Developer Salary," Payscale.com, updated January 12, 2016, accessed September 21, 2016, http://www.payscale.com/research/US/Job=Mobile_Applications_Developer/Salary.

10. "Environmental Science Careers," Environmental Science.org, 2016, accessed August 30, 2016, http://www.environmentalscience.org/careers.

11. "How Will I Know If Engineering Is Right for Me?," Tryengineering.org, 2016, accessed August 10, 2016, http://tryengineering.org/ask-expert/how-will-i-know-if-engineering-right-me.

12. National Association of Colleges and Employers, *Fall 2016 Salary Survey* (Bethlehem, PA: National Association of Colleges and Employers, Fall 2016), 9.

13. Ibid.

14. "Chemical Engineers," *Occupational Outlook Handbook*, 2016–17 ed. (Washington, DC: Bureau of Labor Statistics, December 17, 2015), accessed September 21, 2016, http://www.bls.gov/ooh/architecture-and-engineering/chemical-engineers.htm.

15. "Computer Engineering," Career Cornerstone.org, accessed September 22, 2016, http://www.careercornerstone.org/compeng/compeng.htm.

16. "Professional Land Surveyor Salary," Payscale.com, updated January 12, 2016, accessed September 22, 2016, http://www.payscale.com/research/US/Job=Professional_Land_Surveyor/Salary.

17. National Association of Colleges and Employers, *Winter 2017 Salary Survey*, 9–10.

18. "10 Forensic Myths Spread by TV," Criminal Justice Degrees Guide.com, 2016, accessed August 17, 2016, http://www.criminaljusticedegreesguide.com/features/10-forensic-myths-spread-by-tv.html.

19. "Forensic Accountant Salary," Payscale.com, updated January 12, 2016, accessed September 22, 2016, http://www.payscale.com/research/US/Job=Forensic_Accountant/Salary.

20. "Forensic Pathologist Salary," Payscale.com, updated January 12, 2016, accessed September 22, 2016, http://www.indeed.com/salary/Forensic-Patho logist.html.

21. "Actuary Salary," Payscale.com, updated January 12, 2016, accessed September 22, 2016, http://www.payscale.com/research/US/Job=Actuary/Salary.

22. "Operations Research Analysts," *Occupational Outlook Handbook*, December 17, 2016, accessed January 17, 2017, https://www.bls.gov/ooh/math/opera tions-research-analysts.htm#tab-6.

23. "Job Characteristics," WorldofStatistics.org, 2017, accessed January 16, 2017, http://www.worldofstatistics.org/statistics-as-a-career/job-characteristics.

24. "Statistics Salary," Indeed.com, as of January 19, 2017, accessed January 19, 2017, http://www.indeed.com/salary/Statistics.html.

25. "Mathematician Salary," Payscale.com, updated January 12, 2016, accessed September 22, 2016, http://www.payscale.com/research/US/Job=Mathe matician/Salary.

26. National Association of Colleges and Employers, *Winter 2016 Salary Survey*, 9, 14.

27. Susan Echaore-McDavid, *Career Opportunities in Science* (New York: Ferguson 2003), 2–3.

28. Ibid., 36–37.

29. Ibid., 64–65.

30. "What Does an Oceanographer Do?" *National Ocean Service*, revised June 3, 2014, accessed January 17, 2017, http://oceanservice.noaa.gov/facts /oceanographer.html.

31. Ibid.

32. Matt Rosenberg, "Branches of Geography," About.com, 2017, accessed January 18, 2017, http://geography.about.com/od/studygeography/a/branches geog.htm.

33. "GIS Specialist Salary," Indeed.com, updated January 16, 2017, accessed January 16, 2017, https://www.indeed.com/salary?q1=GIS+Specialist&ll=.

34. Branches of Physics Information," *TechHydra*, 2017, accessed January 17, 2017, http://techhydra.com/science/physics/branches-of-physics.

Chapter 7. Careers for Creative People

1. James Hamblin, "3 Signs You Are Too Creative for a 9–5," *The Atlantic*, accessed August 2, 2016, http://www.theatlantic.com/health/archive/2013/12/3-signs-you-are-too-creative-for-a-9-to-5/282361.

2. Carolyn Gregoire, "18 Things Highly Creative People Do Differently," *The Huffington Post*, March 4, 2016, accessed August 2, 2016, http://www.huffing tonpost.com/2014/03/04/creativity-habits_n_4859769.html.

3. Ibid.

4. Ibid.

5. Molly Owens, "4 Myths about Creative Careers You Probably Believe," Truity.com, August 27, 2015, accessed August 2, 2016, http://www.truity.com /blog/4-myths-about-creative-careers-you-probably-believe.

6. Carol Eikleberry, *The Career Guide for Creative and Unconventional People*, 3rd ed. (Berkeley, CA: Ten Speed Press 2007), 71.

7. Susan H. Haubenstock and David Joselit, *Career Opportunities in Art*, 3rd ed. (New York: Ferguson 2001), 18.

8. "Multimedia Artist or Animator Salary," Payscale.com, updated October 28, 2016, accessed January 17, 2017, http://www.payscale.com/research/US /Job=Multi-Media_Artist_or_Animator/Salary.

9. "Fashion Designer Salary," Payscale.com, updated October 28, 2016, accessed January 17, 2017, http://www.payscale.com/research/US/Job=Fashion_ Designer/Salary.

10. "Creative Director Salary," Payscale.com, updated October 28, 2016, accessed January 17, 2017, http://www.payscale.com/research/US/Job=Creative_ Director/Salary.

11. "Medical Illustrator/Animator," Explore Health Careers.org, 2017, accessed January 19, 2017, http://explorehealthcareers.org/en/Career/87/Medical_ Illustrator__Animator.

12. Dan Drullinger, "Where They Were Before: Steven Spielberg," *Eye of the Intern*, July 12, 2011, http://www.internships.com/eyeoftheintern/news/famous-interns/steven-spielberg.

13. "Spike Lee Biography," *Encyclopedia of World Biography*, 2016, accessed August 2, 2016, http://www.notablebiographies.com/Ki-Lo/Lee-Spike.html#ixz z4HgqTis00.

14. "Script Supervisor Salary in Los Angeles, CA," Indeed.com, as of January 19, 2017, accessed January 19, 2017, http://www.indeed.com/salary?q1=Script+ Supervisor&l1=CA.

15. "Camera Operator, Television and Motion Picture Salaries," Salary.com, as of December 28, 2016, accessed January 19, 2017, http://www1.salary.com /Camera-Operator-Television-and-Motion-Picture-salaries.html.

16. "Become an A&R Coordinator," Careers in Music.com, accessed December 4, 2016, https://www.careersinmusic.com/a-r-coordinator.

17. "Become a Recording Engineer," Careers in Music.com, accessed December 4, 2016, https://www.careersinmusic.com/recording-engineer.

18. Ibid.

19. Shelly Field, *Career Opportunities in the Music Industry* (New York: Ferguson, 2004), 2.

20. Anelia Varela, "There's More to a Career in Writing than Being a Journalist or Novelist," *Guardian Careers*, January 24, 2012, accessed December 4, 2016, https://www.theguardian.com/careers/jobs-journalism-careers.

21. "Editor Salary," Payscale.com, updated October 28, 2016, accessed January 19, 2017, http://www.payscale.com/research/US/Job=Editor/Salary.

22. "Speech Writer Salary," Salary.com, as of December 28, 2016, accessed January 19, 2017, http://www1.salary.com/Speech-Writer-salary.html.

23. Olivia Rubino-Finn, "The Bare Minimum: Breaking down Broadway Actor Salaries," *New Musical Theatre*, January 4, 2016, accessed September 22, 2016, http://newmusicaltheatre.com/greenroom/2016/01/the-bare-minimum-break ing-down-broadway-actor-salaries.

24. "Broadway Actor Salary in New York, NY," Indeed.com, as of September 22, 2016, accessed September 22, 2016, http://www.indeed.com/salary /q-Broadway-Actor-l-New-York,-NY.html.

Chapter 8. Careers for People Who Are Hands-On

1. "Jackson Galaxy Biography," *The Brooks Group*, accessed August 2, 2016, http://www.brookspr.com/clients/jackson-galaxy.

2. "Cesar Millan—Bio," *Cesar's Way*, 2015, accessed August 2, 2016, https:// www.cesarsway.com/cesar-millan/bio.

3. Scott Nolen, "While New Salaries Grow, Debt Remains a Drag," *JAVMA*, May 27, 2015, accessed August 2, 2016, https://www.avma.org/News/JAVMA News/Pages/150615a.aspx.

4. Ibid.

5. Ibid.

6. "Wildlife Biologist Salary," Indeed.com, as of January 19, 2017, accessed January 19, 2017, http://www.indeed.com/salary/Wildlife-Biologist.html.

7. "Horse Trainer Salary," Payscale.com, updated October 28, 2016, accessed January 19, 2017, http://www.payscale.com/research/US/Job=Horse_Trainer /Salary.

8. "Automotive Mechanic I Salaries," Salary.com, as of December 28, 2016, accessed January 19, 2017, http://www1.salary.com/Automotive-Mechanic-I-Salaries.html.

9. "Truck Driver—Tractor Trailer Salaries," Salary.com, as of December 28, 2016, accessed January 19, 2017, http://www1.salary.com/Truck-Driver-Tractor-Trailer-Salaries.html.

10. "Dealership Parts Manager Salary," Indeed.com, as of January 19, 2017, accessed January 19, 2017, https://www.indeed.com/salary?q1=Dealership+Parts+Manager&l1=.

11. "Juvenile Probation Officer Career Guide," Criminal Justice Degree Schools, 2017, accessed January 18, 2017, http://www.criminaljusticedegree schools.com/criminal-justice-careers/juvenile-probation-officer/.

12. "Criminal Justice Jobs," Monster.com, accessed January 18, 2017, http://www.monster.com/jobs/q-criminal-justice-jobs.aspx.

13. "Law Enforcement Salaries," Salary.com, as of December 28, 2016, accessed January 19, 2017, http://www1.salary.com/Law-Enforcement-salaries .html.

14. "Careers outside the Kitchen," Institute of Culinary Education, accessed September 22, 2016, http://www.ice.edu/careers-alumni/careers-outside-the-kitchen.

15. Ibid.

16. Ibid.

17. Ibid.

18. Ibid.

19. G. Stephen Jones, "Career Choices with a Culinary Arts Degree," *The Reluctant Gourmet*, January 24, 2013, http://www.reluctantgourmet.com/careers-culinary-arts-degree.

20. "Culinary Arts Salary Information," All Culinary Schools.com, accessed September 22, 2016, http://www.allculinaryschools.com/culinary-careers/guide /culinary-arts/salaries-for-culinary-arts-careers.

21. "Estimated Probability of Competing in Professional Athletics," NCAA .org, last updated April 25, 2016, accessed August 2, 2016, http://www.ncaa.org /about/resources/research/estimated-probability-competing-professional-athletics.

22. "Athletic Trainer Salaries," Salary.com, as of December 28, 2016, accessed January 19, 2017, http://www1.salary.com/Athletic-Trainer-salaries.html.

Chapter 9. Careers for Organizers

1. Elka Torpey, "Business Careers with High Pay," *Career Outlook* (Washington, DC: Bureau of Labor Statistics, August 2016), accessed August 22, 2016,

http://www.bls.gov/careeroutlook/2016/article/high-paying-business-careers
.htm.

2. Ibid.

3. "Accountants and Auditors," *Occupational Outlook Handbook*, 2016–17 ed. (Washington, DC: U.S. Department of Labor, December 17, 2015), accessed August 11, 2016, http://www.bls.gov/ooh/business-and-financial/accountants-and-auditors.htm.

4. National Association of Colleges and Employers, *Fall 2016 Salary Survey*, 12.

5. "Actuaries," *Occupational Outlook Handbook*, 2016–17 ed. (Washington, DC: U.S. Department of Labor, December 17, 2015), accessed August 11, 2016, http://www.bls.gov/ooh/math/actuaries.htm.

6. "Secretaries and Administrative Assistants," *Occupational Outlook Handbook*, 2016–17 ed. (Washington, DC: U.S. Department of Labor, December 17, 2015), accessed August 11, 2016, http://www.bls.gov/ooh/office-and-administrative-support/secretaries-and-administrative-assistants.htm.

7. "Court Reporters," *Occupational Outlook Handbook*, 2016–17 ed. (Washington, DC: U.S. Department of Labor, December 17, 2015), accessed August 11, 2016, http://www.bls.gov/ooh/legal/court-reporters.htm.

8. "Health Administrator," Explore Health Careers.org, 2017, accessed January 19, 2017, http://explorehealthcareers.org/en/Career/56/Health_Admini strator.

9. "Medical Assistant," Explore Health Careers.org, 2017, accessed January 19, 2017, http://explorehealthcareers.org/en/Career/36/Medical_Assistant.

10. "Medical Records and Health Information Technicians," *Occupational Outlook Handbook*, 2016–17 ed. (Washington, DC: U.S. Department of Labor, December 17, 2015), accessed August 11, 2016, http://www.bls.gov/ooh/health care/medical-records-and-health-information-technicians.htm.

11. "Medical Coder," Explore Health Careers.org, 2017, accessed January 19, 2017, http://explorehealthcareers.org/en/Career/143/Medical_Coder.

12. Ibid.

13. "Medical Records Administrator Salaries," Salary.com, as of December 28, 2016, accessed January 19, 2017, http://www1.salary.com/Medical-Records-Administrator-salary.html.

14. "Medical Scribe Salary," Payscale.com, as of October 28, 2016, accessed January 19, 2017, http://www.payscale.com/research/US/Job=Medical_Scribe/Hourly_Rate.

15. "The Evolving Role of a Medical Transcriptionist," *CareerStep*, June 27, 2016, accessed August 22, 2016, http://www.careerstep.com/blog/medical-trans cription-news/the-evolving-role-of-a-medical-transcriptionist.

16. "Medical Records Transcriptionist Salaries," Salary.com, as of December 28, 2016, accessed January 19, 2017, http://www1.salary.com/Medical-Records-Transcriptionist-salary.html.

17. "Human Resources Assistant I Salaries," Salary.com, as of December 28, 2016, accessed January 19, 2017, http://www1.salary.com/Human-Resources-Assistant-I-Salaries.html.

18. "Human Resources Manager Salaries," Salary.com, as of December 28, 2016, accessed January 19, 2017, http://www1.salary.com/Human-Resources-Manager-Salary.html.

19. Linda P. Carvell, *Career Opportunities in Library and Information Science* (New York: Fergusen, 2005), xi.

20. "Library Science Salary," Indeed.com, as of January 19, 2017, accessed January 19, 2017, http://www.indeed.com/salary?ql=library+science&ll=&tm=1.

Chapter 10. Careers for Persuaders

1. National Association of Colleges and Employers, *Fall 2016 Salary Survey*, 12.

2. "Management Occupations," *Occupational Outlook Handbook*, 2016–17 ed. (Washington, DC: U.S. Department of Labor, December 17, 2015), accessed August 11, 2016, http://www.bls.gov/ooh/Management/home.htm.

3. Dick Lee and Delmar Hatesohl, "Listening: Our Most Used Communications Skill," University of Missouri, accessed January 18, 2017, http://extension.missouri.edu/p/CM150.

4. "Communications Careers," Communications-Major.com, 2017, accessed January 18, 2017, http://www.communications-major.com/careers.

5. "What Is Public Relations?," Communications-Major.com, 2017, accessed January 18, 2017, http://www.communications-major.com/public-relations-managers-and-specialists.

6. National Association of Colleges and Employers, *Fall 2016 Salary Survey*, 8.

7. "Preparing for Law School," American Bar Association, 2016, accessed September 16, 2016, http://www.americanbar.org/groups/legal_education/resources/pre_law.html.

8. Shauna C. Bryce, "Best College Majors and Activities for Aspiring Law School Students," *Career Convergence*, August 1, 2012, http://ncda.org/aws/NCDA/pt/sd/news_article/61758/_PARENT/layout_details_cc/false.

9. "Lawyers," *Occupational Outlook Handbook*, 2016–17 ed. (Washington, DC: U.S. Department of Labor, December 17, 2015), accessed August 11, 2016, http://www.bls.gov/ooh/legal/lawyers.htm.

10. Ibid.

11. National Association of Colleges and Employers, *Fall 2016 Salary Survey*, 12, 20.

12. "Majoring in Political Science," APSANET.org, accessed August 11, 2016, http://www.apsanet.org/CAREERS/Careers-In-Political-Science/Majoring-in-Political-Science2.

13. "Mayor Salary," Payscale.com, updated October 28, 2016, accessed January 19, 2017, http://www.payscale.com/research/US/Job=Mayor/Salary.

14. "Comparison of State Legislative Salaries," Ballotpedia.org, last updated in July 2016, https://ballotpedia.org/Comparison_of_state_legislative_salaries.

15. Ibid.

16. National Association of Colleges and Employers, *Winter 2016 Salary Survey*, 10.

Chapter 11. Gathering Data for Good Decision-Making

1. "Fastest Growing Occupations," *Occupational Outlook Handbook*, 2016–17 ed. (Washington, DC: Bureau of Labor Statistics, December 17, 2015), accessed September 19, 2016, http://www.bls.gov/ooh/fastest-growing.htm.

Chapter 12. Connecting College Majors to Careers

1. C. Andrew, "Crafting a Career Out of Chaos with a Liberal Arts Degree," HackYourWealth.com (blog), accessed July 20, 2016, http://hackyourwealth.com /katharine-brooks-crafting-career-out-of-chaos-with-liberal-arts-degree.

2. "Job Outlook 2016: Attributes Employers Want to See on New College Graduates' Resumes," National Association of Colleges and Employers, November 18, 2015, accessed January 19, 2017, http://www.naceweb.org/s11182015 /employers-look-for-in-new-hires.aspx.

Chapter 13. Making Big Career Decisions

1. "An Overview of Decision-Making Models," Decision-Making-Confi dence.com, accessed July 20, 2016, http://www.decision-making-confidence .com/decision-making-models.html.

2. Ibid.

3. "Blocks to Career Decision Making," *UNSW Australia*, last updated June 21, 2013, accessed October 7, 2016, https://student.unsw.edu.au/blocks-career-decision-making.

4. Herminia Ibarra, *Working Identity: Unconventional Strategies for Reinventing Your Career* (Boston, MA: Harvard Business School Press, 2003), xii.

5. Jordan Weissmann, "Do Unpaid Internships Lead to Jobs? Not for College Students," The Atlantic.com, June 19, 2013, accessed July 25, 2016, http://www .theatlantic.com/business/archive/2013/06/do-unpaid-internships-lead-to-jobs-not-for-college-students/276959.

Chapter 14. What to Do When You're Stuck

1. Molly Owens, "The Upside to Being a Person Who Gets Bored with Everything," Truity.com (blog), June 7, 2016, accessed July 24, 2016, http://www.tru ity.com/blog/upside-being-person-who-gets-bored-everything.

2. Danielle Flug Capalino, "From Fashion to Dietitian: An Unusual Career Path," Nutritioncare.org (blog), accessed August 2, 2016, http://blog.nutrition care.org/from-fashion-to-dietitian-an-unusual-career-path.

Chapter 15. Unique Circumstances

1. Mary E. Ghilani, *10 Strategies for Reentering the Workforce: Career Advice for Anyone Who Needs a Good (or Better) Job Now* (Westport, CT: Praeger, 2009), 25.

2. Brandy L. Smith, "Gay, Lesbian, Bi-Sexual, and Transgender (GLBT) Issues in Advising Situations," *Academic Advising Today*, 2006, accessed October 11, 2016, http://www.nacada.ksu.edu/Resources/Academic-Advising-Today /View-Articles/Gay-Lesbian-Bisexual-and-Transgender-GLBT-Issues-in-Advising-Situations.aspx.

3. Ibid.

4. Ibid.

5. "Personal Competencies for College and Career Success: What Colleges Can Do," National Collaborative on Workforce and Disability for Youth, accessed August 4, 2016, http://www.ncwd-youth.info/PersonalCompetencies.

6. Barbara Bissonnette, "Career Planning for Individuals with Asperger's Syndrome," *Career Convergence*, June 1, 2013, http://careerconvergence.org /aws/NCDA/pt/sd/news_article/73470/_self/CC_layout_details/false.

7. Robert A. Miles, "Career Counseling Strategies and Challenges for Transitioning Veterans," *Career Planning & Adult Development Journal*, 30 no. 3 (Fall 2014): 123–135.

8. Pattie Giordani, "Career Counseling and Hiring Student Veterans," *NACE Journal*, 73, no. 2 (November 2012): 34.

9. "Barred Occupations," *CAREERwise Education*, 2016, accessed September 11, 2016, https://www.careerwise.mnscu.edu/exoffenders/find-job/barred-occupations.html.

10. Ibid.

11. Ibid.

12. Ibid.

Chapter 16. Are You Career Ready?

1. Rosita Smith, "Transferrable Skills," Purdue University Website, accessed October 10, 2016, https://www.purdue.edu/hhs/htm/undergraduate/career_cen ter/documents/career_guide/Transferable_skills.pdf.

2. "Career Readiness Defined," National Association of Colleges and Employers, accessed July 5, 2016, http://www.naceweb.org/knowledge/career-readiness-competencies.aspx.

3. Mary E. Ghilani, *Working in Your Major: How to Find a Job When You Graduate* (Santa Barbara, CA: Praeger, 2012), 152.

4. Ibid.

Index

About the Author

Mary E. Ghilani, MS, NCC, is the director of career services at Luzerne County Community College in Pennsylvania where she provides career counseling and job search services to college students and adults. Her published works include Praeger's *Working in Your Major: How to Find a Job When You Graduate*, *Second Chance: How Career Changers Can Find a Great Job*, and *10 Strategies for Reentering the Workforce: Career Advice for Anyone Who Needs a Good (or Better) Job Now*, as well as numerous career-related articles. Ghilani is a member of the American Counseling Association, the National Career Development Association, and the National Association of Colleges and Employers.